Proven Speed Reading Techniques

Read More Than 300 Pages in 1 Hour. A Guide for Beginners on How to Read Faster with Comprehension (Includes Advanced Learning Exercises)

John R. Torrance, Productivity Coach

YOUR FREE GIFT

This book includes a free bonus booklet. All information on how you can quickly secure your free gift can be found at the end of this book. It may only be available for a limited time.

TABLE OF CONTENTS

INTRODUCTION

How often do you find yourself scrolling through your newsfeed, whether on Facebook or some other news app, and see an article you want to read, but think to yourself: 'I don't have time to read that'? Perhaps you find your reading list piling ever higher with books you haven't read and don't intend to read any time soon. We live in an ever more digitized world with more and more pertinent or interesting information pouring out of everywhere by the second. Our time holds more value than ever. For these reasons, choosing how to spend it becomes a critical decision. Everyone prioritizes their time differently. Some place work-related reading at the top, while others choose politics or other current events. Others still use reading as a way to think about nothing else for a while, a blissful distraction if you will.

Whatever your goal, this book will teach you a secret. You can do all of this, even beyond your current reading goal, with the power of speed reading. Now, you may say that you already read quickly, but let me ask you a couple of things. How often do you find yourself reading something and jumping back a paragraph because you seem to have forgotten every word you just read? Maybe you get hung up on a word or phrase because you do not quite know what it means? Sometimes you might even read to the end of a page or chapter and cannot fully remember what the point was, correct? Speed reading presents a solution to each of these hang-ups and more. By giving you specific pointers to address each concern, there should be no more roadblocks on the journey to speed reading success.

I struggled with reading for a long time. My busy day would enlarge my to-be-read pile, and I'd never get through it all. I nearly gave up, overwhelmed by the reading I wanted to do compared to the time I felt I had. As a productivity coach, however, I needed to press on, and keeping my characteristic look-out for new solutions to boost my efficiency, I stumbled across speed reading. Once I found these easy and effective techniques, I tried and tested them before adopting them in my own reading. My productivity skyrocketed, and I never looked back. Except in particular circumstances, I always speedread, and the amount of reading I did before pales in comparison to the amount I do now.

Writing this book would have taken far more time than it did without the help of speed reading. The hours and hours I spent at the library, surfing the internet, or wracking my brain coming up with ideas or points to include would have taken substantially longer without the ability to read at 1,500 words per minute. Whole books about speed reading became accessible where they previously would not have been. With so many experts on speed reading, each with extensive and well-documented reasons, practices, techniques, and their own tips and tricks, it could have taken months to compose this document. I am proud to say that it took only a couple of weeks. They were busy weeks, do not get me wrong, but I cannot help but praise speed reading for keeping it from taking longer.

So what? You may say, looking for a more tangible or understandable benefit than simply just being able to read faster. Speed reading has numerous other benefits beyond mere consumption of words. Reading faster helps you learn faster, making the time barrier to developing new skills substantially less than before.

Not only will speed reading accelerate your information intake, it might rocket-boost your career as well. The more you read, the more you know, and the more you can share with other people, empowering you in whatever setting you find yourself, work, friends, parties, or anything else.

In addition, speed reading can transform unused hours at the end of the workday into productivity. Taking advantage of this bonus time, you can take an online course for another degree or certification that could advance your job prospects and increase earnings. Your confidence will grow with your understanding of a given topic, thanks to the expansion of your fundamental knowledge. You will also remember a lot more, which may seem strange considering how quickly you will read the information. But with that much more information to take in, naturally, your memory will evolve, particularly as your skills continue to improve.

Do not just take my word for it. Experts back up these claims. Nothing replaces firsthand experience, but the topic of speed reading has naturally enchanted researchers, who spend a great deal of their lives reading.

Some debate whether speed reading inhibits reading accuracy and represents a trade-off. However, scientific studies, such as the one conducted by the University of Michigan Library, concluded that retention improves with the ability to read things faster. A 2016 article in the academic journal *Psychological Science in the Public Interest* analyzed the credibility of speed reading and concluded that speed reading is not a magic bullet. However, *So Much to Read, So Little Time* conceded that there is a substantial improvement in overall speed and effectiveness with key speed reading strategies, only with a trade-off of decreased comprehension.

Luckily, this book has strategies to combat small sacrifices, making them virtual nonfactors. We will hear about tactics from other experts in the speed reading sub-field as well with methods from names such as Scott Young, Jim Kwik, and Evelyn Wood highlighted throughout. If that is not enough, the Internet is littered with experts on anything and everything related to speed reading or otherwise. You will hear from several of them, including Ron Cole, Jordan Harry, Jim Kwik, and Tim Ferriss, as they testify to the benefits of speed reading. With my own experiences and the backing of peer-reviewed research, this book will serve as a primer to the speed reading neonate.

How much exactly will these tips and tricks help? For reference, the average person reads about 200-300 words per minute. Does this seem good to you? Before you come up with your opinion, what if I told you that you could read 1,500 words per minute or more? Most speed reading experts cap the upper limits of their word processing speed at 500-600 words per minute, calling it the most you can realistically read without a serious sacrifice to retention. However, world speed reading champions, like Anne Jones can routinely read at upwards of 3,000 words per minute. Jones set the record at 4,700 words per minute with a retention rate of 67 percent. I cannot make you a world record holder in the shadow of Anne Jones, but you will get closer to her rate than the limited rates of other experts. I can promise that with the information and exercises contained in this book, you can count 1,500 words per minute as a baseline. With ample time and practice, you may even exceed that expectation. Who knows, you could possibly be the next world champion speed reader. Just do not let that be your realistic expectation.

Here is the progression of the next ten chapters.

Chapter one will detail the benefits of speed reading. They are numerous and far reaching, anything from increasing your reading output to expanding your memory and comprehension. This chapter will lay the groundwork for your expectations as far as what you will get out of this book. If you do not like what you read here, you can put the book down, but I doubt that will be the case.

Chapter two tackles three misconceptions about speed reading. I am not entirely certain how they developed, but they seem to have taken on a sizable following in popular culture. Speed reading seems like a superpower, especially for literal superheroes in fiction that claim to read 10,000 words per minute. It is ludicrous. The second involves subvocalization and the falsehood that you need to get rid of it to read fast. Also not true. Lastly, reading automatically helps you read faster. Again, not true. This chapter will dispel these myths

Chapter three charges you to embrace whatever level at which you currently read. By breaking down where you stand now, you can honestly develop things you want to work on throughout the book. Bearing in mind how you read and what kind of reader you are lets you move forward with making yourself a better one.

Chapter four introduces you to a basic tenet of speed reading, calculating your speed. By following the formula you can set a quantitative baseline for your reading. Remember this technique down the line. It will come in handy as you try to measure your reading speed and its progression.

Chapter five launches you headfirst into improving your reading speed, by giving you the tips and tricks you need to start out. It involves goal setting, first and foremost, to moderate your expectations for your improvement, ensuring that you find the right balance of ambition and realism. It includes skimming, the most well-known speed reading technique. Other tactics, such as stopping subvocalization, reading phrases, meta-guiding, Rapid Serial Visual Presentation, will build your speed reading foundation.

Chapter six will calm any fears you may have about sacrificing comprehension for speed, something opponents of speed reading will use to base their arguments. Reading comprehension goes beyond just taking in the words and understanding them. It extends to visualization, expanding your vocabulary, and other active reading strategies. Speed reading can lead to a small sacrifice in retention, but the practices in this chapter will help you mitigate those losses substantially. Reading quickly doesn't necessarily impair your comprehension.

Chapter seven will acknowledge that the underlying basis for getting better at reading lies in simply doing it more. You will develop familiarity with the things you read, as well as routines and habits that will lend themselves to your continued reading. The crucial first step in becoming a master speed reader is establishing a strong base.

Chapter eight deals with the problem of keeping track of your reading and giving you structure to document your habits. It recommends tried and true methods while conceding that times have changed and new ones exist that can help you just as much as the old ones. It matters much less how you keep track of your reading than the fact that you do. It helps you maintain focus on your goals and makes you feel good about your progress, regardless of the rate at which it comes. The best way to keep track of that? Time your reading using the formula in chapter four every so often. That will give you verifiable data to follow and let you analyze it however you want.

Chapter nine takes a deep dive into one of the most popular and successful speed reading tactics. Skimming and scanning sound like cheap cop-outs due to the connotations they have taken on, but, in reality, they help you identify and acquire the most important parts of the reading. We will not give away too much in the introduction, but they require a much more active and engaged reading style that you may have previously assumed.

Lastly, **chapter ten** will give you the inside scoop on the most advanced reading techniques, straight from the experts like yours truly. At first glance, they may seem identical to methods in chapter five, but it would be more appropriate to refer to them as extensions of the methods in chapter five. The chapter discusses one of the first speed reading experts, Evelyn Wood, from whom you can learn about one of the more bizarre things to happen on a college campus in the 1960s.

Think of the smartest people you know, whether from popular culture or from your workplace or family life. Do you envy them for the sheer amount of things they know? Do you wish that you could do and say the things they do? Do you want to show off your newfound knowledge to get even, perhaps finally claiming victory at your weekly trivia? Speed reading can be the weapon that keeps you in the intellectual arms race of sorts. If you keep reading this book, you too can unlock the superpower of knowledge and give yourself an edge in whichever form you want it to manifest. All it takes is small tweaks to your current practices and habits, the ones I mention in this book. With them, you will be able to exponentially improve your daily information consumption.

However you want to think about it, whether in terms of words per minute gained, improved comprehension, or time saved, speed reading techniques will make you a better reader. They will do all of those things and more, transforming your reading time from the chore it could have been previously to something you enjoy doing because of the feeling you get or the skills or knowledge you obtain. In purchasing this book you have taken the first step to capitalizing on the promise of considerable potential.

CHAPTER ONE:

How Will Increasing Your Reading Speed Help You?

Let us begin with a thought experiment. Think about all of the required reading you have to do on a given day. Include all of the emails, texts, social media scrollings, news articles, briefings, or any other reading you may do on that day. How much time would you save if you could do it in a third of the time you take now? Or even more ambitiously, what if it took only a fifth of the time it does now? It seems almost too good to be true, does it not? Not quite a superpower out of a Marvel or DC Comic book, but certainly something to strive for. This ability would alter the course of many of our lives.

Quickly reading and comprehending books, articles, and other materials with retention of quality would enable us to round out our perspectives and broaden the scope of our understanding. Armed with this newfound capacity to know things, personal success in whichever form you choose would come more easily. Career paths would move quicker with promotions or raises following your increased productivity in the workplace. Businesses would operate more quickly and effectively. You might even be able to make more lasting first impressions after demonstrating how knowledgeable you are. This book will help you in these ways and more.

In what should not surprise anyone at all, this book will make you a speed reader. With the tips and tricks in this book, you will read more in less time. Your improvement could manifest itself in a doubling or tripling of your current reading speed. You will learn to skim, overstepping information of lesser significance to land only on crucial information.

We will dive into it in more detail later, but there is a misconception about skimming. Some view it as just quickly passing over all of the information on the page without fully engaging with it. This could not be more false. Skimming does involve reading a lot of information quickly, but the process is much more active than that. Skimming relies on a thorough preview of whatever you decide to read, picking out key words, phrases, and ideas to pay attention to while you read. Your eyes pick up on these valuable points, allowing you to skip over anything you may not deem important enough, such as examples. This way your brain is primed to pick up the same important information in less time.

Many people consider speed reading a hack of sorts, something that improves your life so much that it seems like cheating. Few people, though, recognize how exactly it can help, other than reading fast. The lifestyle website *Life Hack* posted an article entitled "10 Reasons Why You Should Learn Speed Reading", and gave some broad and specific examples of just that. Ranging from empowerment to enhanced problem-solving skills, the article offers plenty of justification for the skill. It says that as an empowering skill, speed reading boosts your comfort level wherever you may be, since it allows you to read up on more topics and therefore sound smarter when you talk. Particularly at parties, it gives you more to talk about and makes your opinions smarter, since they are based on more facts and less on speculation. It can make you smarter in a more tangible sense as well since you can turn your newfound ability to consume higher quantities of information and translate that information to certifications or degrees. Think you do not have time for that master's degree or program you keep putting off? Speed reading could be the difference in the equation and make you more money as a result.

Speed Reading Improves Confidence

In addition to more comfortable and better educated, speed reading can make you more confident, particularly in the workplace. If you spend your time and newfound reading capabilities brushing up on anything and everything related to your job, you will get better at it. And the comfort you exude at parties will factor in discussions with your boss as well. In that situation, and any where you may encounter resistance from an argumentative standpoint, you will calmly and easily respond with something you remember from your speed reading.

Speed Reading Augments Memory

Speaking of which, you will remember a lot more after learning to speed read. It makes sense since your reading ability and comprehension is a function of how well you can remember what you read. While there's definitely a requisite amount of memory capability you need in order to read in general, reading more, especially faster, helps train your brain. Reading will facilitate more connections between information and memory in your brain, making it easier to quickly conjure up useful facts or knowledge. How nice would it be to remember something you are supposed to do, whatever it may be, without the jump-out-of-bed panic that often accompanies poor memory? Not only that, your augmented memory can make you more creative, as well.

Speed Reading Quickens Learning

Of course, the most obvious benefit of speed reading is that it enables you to learn more quickly. Spending less time per read means you can read more. Reading more means learning more. Part and parcel with that is sophistication. You are smarter, more comfortable and confident, better educated, and can retain more, that helps your brain tremendously in creating new synapses, or connections between brain cells. The more neural pathways your brain can utilize and the stronger they are, the better you will get at the sheer act of thinking.

Speed Reading Hones Focus and Decreases Stress

Related to that, the act of thinking, particularly with the kind of focus that speed reading requires, can induce meditative qualities. Think about when you are in the zone, in any application, be it sports, work, art, quite literally anything. That feeling when all else drops away and you can focus your entire attention on one task? Speed reading tends to induce that. Not only will this help you focus, but it also has serious stress-relieving qualities as well. This leads to an overall improvement in emotional well-being. Given the relaxing nature of reading, it reduces stress and takes your mind off of worries and other intrusive thoughts that neither benefit nor increase your health. The material absorbs you when you read faster, promoting focus on the information you are reading more than anything else. As an act of active meditation, you achieve the same meditative state as a Buddhist monk.

Speed Reading Opens Up Career Opportunities

Naturally, a decrease in stress allows you to focus on more important things, such as your career. Do you think Bill Gates or his ilk let stress stop them from becoming some of the greatest innovators to live? The ability to limit stress, whether as a result of saved time from speed reading or something else, presents a significant quality of life boost. The clarity of mind that it affords enhances problem-solving capabilities, for example. The best ideas are often instincts, according to this logic, and speed reading helps develop those instincts.

Speed Reading Increases Logic and Problem Solving Skills

Of course, a critical component of problem solving is logic. Your ability to think logically also increases with speed reading. Just think shortly on the goals of speed reading. You've got to understand swaths of information quickly. In order to do as much, you must logically sort information into two pools: important and unimportant. Doing so as quickly as speed reading requires will undoubtedly improve your ability to think and process logically.

A Couple Misconceptions About Speed Reading

You will find yourself laser-focused on whatever you read. Most people have the ability to read at 200 words per minute, with some logging higher counts at about 300 words per minute. Many readers have a misconception that in order to focus more on what you are reading, you need to slow down and digest every word. This is false for two reasons.

First, traditional reading styles and the methods through which they are taught lack efficiency.

Second, people read slowly due to a lack of focus. Think about it. How many distractions do you have when you sit down to read a book? The most salient distraction is probably in your pocket as you read this. When your phone buzzes, it's almost as if the world around it pauses for a moment, does it not? It could be anything: a text, a Facebook notification, a like on your Instagram photos, updates to your Twitter feed, an email from your boss, or simply a dank meme. Whatever it is, our highly connected lives limit the capacity for quiet. You can scarcely catch a moment of uninterrupted time. However, the focus required to speed read makes this point moot. You haven't got the time to be distracted.

And again, we circle back to some of the main benefits of speed reading. If focus is improved, so too are comprehension, memory, and retention of information. The brain is like a muscle. If we train our brains in this way, they will grow stronger and perform better. Speed reading challenges our brains to perform at a higher level. When you train your brain to be able to take in information faster, other areas of your brain will also improve.

What Do the Detractors Say?

A quick google search will yield all sorts of articles and testimonies about how speed reading isn't all it's cracked up to be. Opponents will argue that reading at such high speeds reduces comprehension. Some contend that the human eye and brain cannot coordinate to process words and sentences quickly enough to make much more than 600 words per minute attainable. These studies are well funded and founded, your brain doesn't in fact operate quickly enough for traditional reading methods to function at that speed.

How Can That Be?

So doesn't that make this book a waste of time? No. The techniques contained in this book will teach you how to account for the fact that traditional reading methods don't suffice for 1,500 words per minute reading speeds. There are many studies, similar in authenticity and integrity to opposing ones, that confirm the legitimacy of reading at high speeds. It dates to 1950 when the University of Nebraska conducted a study of 150 business students about speed reading. Don Clifton, chair of the psychology department, divided the students into two groups, one called Gifted with a 350 words per minute average reading speed. The other so-called Normal group clocked in at 90 words per minute. Each group was given the same speed reading course, to varied reactions from faculty, worried that it would corrupt the Gifted students. The Normal group showed significant improvement, increasing to 150 words per minute. That 66 percent increase paled in comparison to the Gifted group, which shot up to 2,900 words per minute, an increase of 828 percent.

You'll notice the extremely high reading speed as well as the percentage increase and that this book offers something lower. Maybe you'll discredit that study as evidence. That's okay because there are plenty more. Take, for instance, the University of Utah study conducted by Leann Larsen, entitled *Does Speed Reading Improve College Student's Retention Level and Comprehension?*. Basing her analysis on three articles that this book will discuss later, she hypothesized that students who learn to speed read gain comprehension of more material and retainment of the information better compared to the students who do not. John Macalister of the Victoria University of Wellington in New Zealand concluded that speed reading does in fact increase student's reading speeds, even when the text is authentic, or new to them. *Speed reading courses and their effect on reading authentic texts: A preliminary investigation* focuses less on retention, but acknowledges that retention was a critical component to the study and was maintained even with high speeds.

Speed Reading Makes Reading More Enjoyable Overall

Naturally, we enjoy doing things we are good at, and with improved reading skills, reading will transform from something we feel obligated to do into something we enjoy. When we enjoy doing things, we put more effort and energy into getting better at them, whether we realize it or not. This book will engage you with advanced learning techniques. Want to learn a new language? Speed reading helps you discover and navigate the grammatical and vocabulary nuances of whichever language you choose. Want to incorporate a new business skill into your work? Similarly, speed reading makes refresher or augmenting courses much more accessible. You can even increase your value to an employer.

Speed Reading Helps Eliminate Bad Habits

Lastly, think about how many bad habits you have formed. It takes conscious and dedicated efforts to unlearn them and replace them, and even more practice and discipline to keep up the new habits without developing more bad ones. Speed reading presents an opportunity to discover and replace bad habits you may have. These stem from your elementary education. Everyone had a teacher that they did not particularly like or realized in hindsight failed at his or her job. How would you like them to have a profound impact on your past, present, and future? I can't imagine anyone would, especially if they were not popular.

This book makes these examples as well as many others realistic. To take the most advantage of these tips and tricks, I recommend you have the following materials handy when doing exercises in this book: Pencil or pen, highlighter, paper, calculator, watch or stopwatch, and, of course, your book or reading material.

More Than That, Speed Reading Makes You a Better Reader

Before you dismiss this as obvious and move on, let me explain. Of course, it will make your reading faster. Beyond that, though, speed reading, in the form of the techniques included in this book, will give you tactics that you can use to make your reading more efficient. For the purposes of this book, I want you to use them at high speeds. However, you can still use them at any speed you like. Paul Nation wrote an article about just this, with an emphasis on language fluency. Somewhat elemental, *Reading Faster* noted that recognizing letters leads to faster processing of words, and so too recognizing words faster processing of sentences and ideas. Continuing this building block, he analyzed how simple sentences turn into complex sentences. This increases not only speaking and writing but reading too. Nation brought up two core techniques which this book will address in the coming chapters, skimming and scanning. He differentiated skimming as reading a text quickly, aiming for acquiring the big picture of what it is about, at the expense of some details. Scanning, on the other hand, requires the reader to seek out specific information, in the form of names or numbers. Nation acknowledges the merits of each but concedes that skimming offers more benefit than scanning, for ease of use, in the pursuit of language fluency. As a summarization, Nation posits that skimming represents the next building block in the development of language fluency and results in a more proficient ability to read it, along with the other functions of writing and speaking.

Chapter Summary

- You can cut the amount of time you currently spend reading substantially.
- You can fill that time with more reading, multiplying the amount of effective reading time in your day.

- More than just time spent and amount of reading, speed reading comes with other benefits and byproducts, like career advancement and skill development.
- Speed reading combats ineffective traditional reading styles and discredits the assumption that slower reading is more focused and effective.
- Speed reading promotes focus because it requires and facilitates a concerted effort to consume and retain information as quickly and accurately as possible.
- Speed reading challenges the brain and strengthens it, and, in the same way as a bicep or other muscle exercise, also supports and strengthens other parts of the brain.
- Speed reading will help you enjoy reading and make you better at it.
- Speed reading reveals the opportunity to learn new skills at a faster pace.

The next chapter will debunk myths you may have been taught about reading faster. With the support of evidence, chapter two will alleviate your reservations and misconceptions about speed reading with thorough research.

3 Myths You Were Taught About Reading Faster

While there are many misconceptions about speed reading, some exceed the scope of myth. This chapter will dispel 3 popularized myths about speed reading to further convince you that speed reading is real, effective, and can benefit you tremendously. They exaggerate what speed reading is, looks like, and does for you. Without further ado, here are the 3 biggest myths about reading faster.

Myth #1: You can read 10,000 words per minute

Let us put this one into mathematical perspective. 10,000 words with Times New Roman at 12 pt font size, the same as this text here, with single spacing, is 20 pages, and with double spacing is 40 pages. With 500 words and 250 words on each page respectively. Also, 10,000 words per minute reduces to 166 ⅓ words per second, making the rate about a page or half a page per second. Scientific studies show that the brain typically processes images, not words, in about 100 milliseconds. In a

2014 study conducted by Massachusetts Institute of Technology, neuroscientists found that the eye needs as little as 13 milliseconds to process concepts as shown in images. Applying both of these calculations, that amounts to 16 ⅓ words per 100 millisecond and 2 ⅙ words per 13 milliseconds. Those speeds are quite literally lightning-fast and frankly unattainable, particularly when considering the difficulty of picking words out of a sentence, paragraph, or page.

Think about it like this. This book is roughly 30,000 words. Do you think you could realistically read a third of this book in a minute? It's absurd. That's not what speed reading is about.

These processes, unlike the processing of images displayed in the MIT study, require the movement and refocusing of the eye, substantially lengthening the time required to read and comprehend the information. The assertion that the human brain can read at 10,000 words makes for great imagery in movies or TV. Superheroes like Superman, The Flash, and Quicksilver might be able to do it. But there is a reason that this is, for the most part, fiction. Only superhumans possess this ability. 10,000 words per minute is simply impossible, as Calvin of *Calvin and Hobbes* famously says, "reading is easy if you do not sweat comprehension."

Myth #2: Subvocalization Impedes Speed Reading

For those of you who may be unfamiliar, subvocalization is the voice you hear in your head while you read. Some speed reading experts contend that the elimination of subvocalization is the key to speed reading. Scott Young, however, admits that while this does enhance your ability to process words more quickly, the tradeoff involves a marked decrease in comprehension. So how then, if you do not eliminate subvocalization, can you possibly hope to read faster? With subvocalization critical to reading comprehension, the fastest readers quite simply are better at it and do it faster. As a testament to the efficacy of this practice, NASA constructed a system to register these impulses in order to browse the web or control a spacecraft. In exactly the same process that subvocalization will help you learn a new language, it facilitates your reading comprehension.

Myth #3: Reading Is the Same as Practicing Speed Reading

One might think that the simple act of reading enables us to read faster. However, like any practice, if we do not correctly implement the techniques or methods intentionally, we develop bad habits that we often do not recognize. In the name of full or over-comprehension, we can reread sentences or paragraphs, or get fixated on words or phrases we are unfamiliar with. Furthermore, unless you actively stretch your normal reading speed, you are not practicing speed reading.

But wait, you may say, those best-selling, page-turning novels I read beg to differ! Your point would be valid so long as you account for the fact that these books are intended to be read quickly. They rely on simple concepts, comprehension, and vivid imagery to advance the plot and thematic points they write about. Also, how often do you read a book like that, or any other for that matter, and remember the whole thing? Practicing speed reading requires a little sacrifice of retention at first.

Continued, mindful practice will in time improve your retention as well, but expecting speed and comprehension to improve simultaneously is perhaps overly optimistic. As such, when you are reading, do so for the purpose of enjoyment. To improve your speed reading, dedicate specific time to improve the speed at which you read.

Chapter Summary

- Because of the somewhat mysterious and seemingly unattainable nature, speed reading myths exist and tend to further mystify it or make it seem more inaccessible.
- These myths exist because speed reading appears too good to be true.
- The first one is hyperbole, that people can read as many as 10,000 words per minute.
- The second myth is that you must eliminate subvocalization, the inner voice in your head when you read, in order to achieve realistic levels of speed reading.
- Lastly, people do not naturally improve their speed reading just by reading normally.

Now that we have established the benefits of speed reading and discredited falsehoods about it, let us start to talk about your expectations for your own reading and speed reading. You may have visions of yourself blazing through all manner of reading. First, though, we need to find a baseline. This next chapter will figure out where you are now with your speed reading.

CHAPTER THREE:

Embrace Your Level of Reading

Just like any other skill, beginning to learn speed reading requires honesty about your current abilities. You would never walk into a gym or weight lifting class and start trying to bench press 300 or more pounds on your first try. If you were an aspiring actor or actress, you would never step onto a set for a movie for which you hadn't rehearsed lines. If you're an artist, you'd never find your first painting in a museum next to a Picasso. You get the point.

In the same way, you need to acknowledge and embrace the fact that you may be a beginner speed reader. You'll undoubtedly have goals to strive for on day one, but you need to let go of the idea of being a master at day 1. If you, as you do right now, read at about 200 words per minute, it will take more than the amount of work you can put in in one day to build up and maintain a reading speed of 1,500 words per minute. With that bit of tough love behind us, we all start somewhere, and wherever that place may be, it is okay, especially since by purchasing this book you have chosen to improve. Nonetheless, like anything else in life, in order to know where you are going, you have to know where to start. Set lofty goals or expectations for yourself, but understand that it is not easy and may not come as quickly as you would like. In that case, do not be hard on yourself, just keep working.

Let us analyze a bit more where you are right now. How would you describe yourself as a reader? What things do you like to read most? What things can you not stand reading? What things would you like to read more? Are there certain things you would like to get through faster when you read? Are there things you want to better understand when you read them? Most importantly but not quite as obviously, examine the explanations for your answers. Why do you say or do these things?

Fun fact, did you know that reading is not a natural human biological function? That is right, unlike things we often associate with reading, like seeing, hearing, feeling, or even language, our brains do not naturally know how to read. Instead, humans acquired reading as a skill and developed it culturally. Dr. Yuval Noah Harari explains the evolution of reading and writing from its foundation as an accounting for grain storages and purchases in his book *Sapiens: A Brief History of Humankind.* By co-opting other developed cognitive strategies such as image recognition and linguistic parsing, language first incorporated things that could be touched, seen, heard, smelled, or tasted. Concrete ideas such as these eventually allowed for abstract ideas to be communicated, such as religions, myths, fantasies, or legends. This created a sharp juxtaposition between the physical reality we all share and the imagined reality each of us inhabits ourselves.

It took many thousands of years, until roughly the Agricultural Revolution, before writing was invented and, with it, reading. A process we utilize on a daily basis and take for granted actually comes from a long and complicated history. Reading and writing are difficult and somewhat unnatural to humans. Otherwise, global literacy rates would be higher than the 86.31%, as the current figure cited by the World Bank stands. You might look at this percentage and exclaim, "Wow, that's pretty good." And it is. It's better than it has ever been in recorded history. Still, it demonstrates a critical fact: Reading is not an innate, instinctive skill.

Beyond the esoteric, meta-historical perspective, there are more tangible constraints to improving your speed reading. Feel free to blame any one or number of them if you get frustrated. Most broadly, not knowing the topic might have the greatest effect on your ability to read quickly. Abstract and difficult to understand topics will almost assuredly slow your pace as you grapple with the content at hand. Secondly, not knowing the words will also slow you down. The more words you do not know, the more you will have to scratch your head trying to figure out what it means before your stubbornness frustrates you into consulting a dictionary. Lastly, not knowing the sounds will impede your reading progress. This bit isn't particularly common in your native language, but it does happen every once in a while. Loan words from other languages have the potential to stump you while you read, in the same way that learning other languages would. Conversely, the more about the topic, words, and sounds you know, the more your speed reading will increase.

Chapter Summary

- Before you can access where you want to go, you need to know where you are now, speed reading is no different than anything else that way.

- Think about yourself as a reader. That is the best way to determine your stepping off point when wanting to speed read better.

- Understand that reading is not something you should take for granted and is actually foreign to the human biological default hardware settings. Your ancestors developed it in a complicated process millennia ago.

- More relevantly, there are constraints to your reading. Not knowing the topic, words, or sounds in the reading can impede your progress.

- On the flip side, increased knowledge of the topic, words, and sounds will make your reading easier.

Now we have established an abstract baseline of sorts, based on your own descriptions of yourself as a reader and the understanding that reading is difficult and complicated. In the next chapter, you will undertake a more quantitative assessment of your fundamental skills as a reader by calculating your reading speed. This will turn your abstract goal of wanting to generally read faster into a recognizable goal of exactly how much faster you want to read compared to your current reading speed.

CHAPTER FOUR:

How to Calculate Your Reading Speed

If you are trying to increase your reading speed, then you need to keep track of what it is. This calculation was developed for students taking the LSAT, the standardized test for those who wish to get into law school. Follow the instructions to get a good estimate of your effective reading speed.

The Formula

Estimate the number of words on a page by counting the number of words in two lines and dividing by two. So if there are 37 words in two lines, then the word count per line is 18.5.

Count the number of lines on the page page. Multiply by the number of words per line. So, if there are 50 lines on a page, 50 x 18.5 = 925 words on a page.

If you want to be even more accurate, you can simply use software to check the number of words on a particular eBook page.

Read a page. Count how long it takes in seconds.

Divide the words per page by the seconds it took you to read the page. Multiply by 60 to get the words per minute. For the purpose of this exercise let us say it took you four minutes and 30 seconds to read the page. That amounts to 270 seconds. 925 divided by 270 is equal to 3.425. That times 60 is about 205 words per minute.

Let's repeat that formula and simplify here. Determine the words per line (WPL). Next, determine the lines per page (LPP). Multiply WPL by LPP to get the words per page (WPP). Now get your stopwatch. Start it. Read the page. Convert the time to seconds. Divide the WPP by the seconds. Multiply by 60 to get your words per minute (WPM).

One more time, the formula is as follows:

WPM = WPP (LPP x WPL) / Seconds x 60

Now you can calculate your own WPM (reading speed), but before you do so, take a couple of steps to ensure you're focused:

- Find a quiet spot to read alone
- Eliminate distractions (TVs, cell phones, browser tabs, etc.)
- Make sure you're comfortable
- Have your stopwatch and book at the ready

Got all that? Now calculate your own reading speed and write the figure somewhere so you can track your progress as you read this book.

Periodically, measure the speed at which you read. Ideally, you should use the same book, or at least the same author, to standardize the test. Otherwise, you would get an inaccurate estimate of your reading speed. Reading the same book will ensure that you are not reading faster or slower due to the difficulty of the book to read. It can also be a book you have already read. In fact, that may be better than a book you have not read because, at least in theory, you should know all of the words in the book.

After conducting the test and calculating your own reading speed, see where you stand below. These figures were taken from a study sponsored by Staples to market for an e-book and were cited in a Forbes magazine article. Use this information only as a benchmark to evaluate where you are. Do not get discouraged if the result is not what you want, because by reading this far into the book, you have demonstrated a good commitment to improving your reading speed. With time and practice, your speed should see a considerable increase.

- The average reading speed of an adult is 300 words per minute.
- A typical third-grade student reads at a rate of 150 wpm (words per minute).
- Eighth grade students can usually achieve speeds of 250 wpm.
- Your average college student will hit about 450 wpm.
- An average "high-level executive" takes in about 575 wpm for their super important corporate job.
- Given the high level of education required of their job (usually a doctoral degree), an average college professor reads at 675 wpm so that they can get through all of the immeasurable amounts of work their students produce and still meet grading deadlines.
- Speed readers can reach limits of 1,500 wpm or more, particularly with the help of speed reading books such as this.

- We already mentioned her, but Anne Jones is worth mentioning again. As a World speed reading champion, she reaches an astounding 4,700 wpm.

Chapter Summary

- Calculating your reading speed is easy. Following the formula, you can determine reading speed in five minutes or less.
- Estimate the words per page by counting the words in two lines and then dividing by two.
- Count the number of lines per page then multiply by words per line.
- Alternatively, for those reading electronic books, highlight all the text on the page and check the word count using your e-reader or copy and paste the words into a word count checker.
- Read a page and count the number of seconds it takes.
- Divide the words per page by the seconds it took to get words per second.
- Multiply by 60 to get your words per minute.
- That formula can be represented as such: WPM = WPP (LPP x WPL) / Seconds x 60
- Regularly repeat the exercise to log your progress, using the same book, ideally.
- Use the information above as a reference for your speed reading level and a baseline to compare your progress to once you have practiced for some time.

Congratulations! You now know exactly where you stand as a speed reader. By this point in the book, you have heard a lot about the benefits of speed reading and some myths associated with it. You have established an idea of who you are as a reader and calculated your words per minute. You may be wondering when you will get to the good stuff, exactly how to improve your speed reading. Luckily, the next chapter will be the first that reveals tips and tricks about how to do just that.

CHAPTER FIVE:

How to Read Faster

Have a Goal

The first step to speed reading actually happens before you even really start to read a book, article, essay, or anything else you may choose. This involves setting a goal for what you read. Namely, what do you want to get out of whatever you are about to read? Do you want to learn about the latest in current events in a newspaper article? Or perhaps learn a new skill like you are right now? Maybe you picked up the latest bestseller that everyone is talking about and you want to check it out for yourself. The exact reason or goal does not matter nearly as much as the act of setting one. Having a goal in mind when you read helps you tremendously as you read. It keeps you focused on why you are reading. It helps you hunt down particular knowledge while you read, and alerts you when you need to slow down and focus for certain, crucial passages, maximizing your comprehension.

Do Something While You Read

What, like multi-task? Should I be trying to get chores done while I have a book in my hands? No, that's not what I'm suggesting. A lot of the struggles associated with general reading as well as speed reading come with a passive approach to it. By that I mean, you do nothing more than move your eyes over the words and try to comprehend them. In his book, *Breakthrough Rapid Reading*, Peter Kump hones in on this passivity, remedying this by prescribing active involvement with whatever it is you're doing, in this case reading. This maximizes your conscious concentration and reinforces your understanding of what you read. Quoting psychologist William James, he assesses that improving memory involves improving the habits we use to record facts. From this, Kump surmises that active reading and organization while throughout improves the ways in which you record or receive information. That's not enough though. Kump says that in order to make the information yours, you have to use it and apply it in some way. Whether that's repeating it or synthesizing it in conjunction with something else, you don't own it unless you do. This chapter will show you some ways you can apply this reasoning to your reading to take advantage of the benefits of active reading.

The Magic of Skimming

Modulating your reading speed helps readers get the most out of their reading while also increasing the speed at which they read. We call this technique skimming. By selectively reading information that you deem most important and glossing over unnecessary things, skimming can be incredibly effective once we determine the information we wish to obtain from a given text. Skimming can serve another purpose as well. Quickly reading the text over before you examine it closer helps your eye and your brain pick up on the information that interests you most. This familiarizes you with it in general before you commit to reading it in depth. A study found that this practice increases comprehension noticeably.

Think about the last time you studied for an exam. I realize it may have been quite some time ago for some, but bear with me nonetheless. When preparing for an exam or a big presentation, if you prefer, your time is limited. So naturally, you skip over any information that would not help you and begin with the most important. We quickly skimmed through the exam papers to figure out and understand the structure of it, what kind of questions would be on it, and which parts were worth the most points. From there we could maneuver the exam quicker and more efficiently because we knew where the biggest gains and losses were to be had. For instance, if an essay question was worth just as much as the multiple choice and short answer portions combined, we may start with the essay before getting to the fewer-points-per-question areas. In reading anything, generally, we find the most important information in the introduction and the conclusion. Taking this strategy, reading those parts while skimming anything in between would best serve us in terms of information retained.

Consider Replacements for Subvocalization

Here is where a modulation in subvocalization can help substantially. When skimming, we already sacrifice retention for speed because the information is not as important to us. Because we have already accepted this, we can stop subvocalizing as much to assist us in speeding through these sections. In instances such as this one, subvocalization is the primary factor, by far, in slowing down our reading. It grinds our reading speed down to about 300 words per minute. The pace of a snail, about a fifth of our potential! Your eyes and brain can process information at a much faster rate. Stopping that narrator in your head from slowing you down can double your effective reading speed pretty quickly.

Hold on a second there, you might say, it is much easier said than done. This is true, stopping subvocalization can be difficult, especially if you feel like you have to subvocalize to read effectively. It is definitely quite the trick, and it took me quite some time to kick this habit. Psychologically speaking, it is incredibly hard to stop habits. However, it is fairly easy to replace one habit with another. Rather than grinding your teeth and trying to stop subvocalizing, distract yourself somehow. Use your finger or a pencil to follow the words, listen to music or your favorite podcast, or chew gum while you read.

Learn to Group Words While Reading

Another difficult habit to overcome is reading each individual word one at a time. We were taught in school that in order to understand a whole sentence that we have to understand the meaning of each word. Even though the last time we last heard a lesson like that was potentially a very long time ago, we still hold its value as true. How often, though, do you read a sentence where you do not know more than one or two of the words? Even if you do, you can usually figure out what these unknown words mean through context clues. Using the same technique of reading a few words around one to figure out what it means, you can read a few words at a time to increase your reading speed.

You can do that because your eye spans about 1.5 inches, more than enough to read five words, maybe three or four if they are shorter. The better you get, the more you can increase this span, with up to nine words in it, working wonders for your reading speed. Again, this may seem easier said than done, but if you focus on every fifth word or so, the results may surprise you. This does take some training before you can fully take advantage of this skill. Like anything, time and practice improve it. I would caution you against using it for anything important, like a textbook, before you feel fully comfortable with it, though.

The article I mentioned earlier, "So Much to Read, So Little Time", addressed this phenomenon directly. It details how significantly acuity limits vision and constrains the reading process, inhibiting retention beyond the fovea, the center point of vision and the location where fixation occurs. This area constitutes up to 1 degree in any direction of the angle of vision away from it and provides the highest acuity compared to the parafovea 1 degree to 5 degrees away from the center of vision. The rest of the field of vision is the periphery and has little acuity. While the article contends that acuity decreases the further from the center of vision, some retention is still possible, as illustrated by the picture that follows. While the words blur more toward the ends of the sentences, they are still legible, and for the purposes of speed reading, can still be retained for higher speed reading rates. It is scientifically true that word recognition occurs most often and effectively in the fovea, but some does occur outside of it. For a deeper analysis of why that is, refer to the article for a description of how rods and cones in the eye work. Unfortunately, we do not have time for such a thing here.

As a part of his Backpack Series, Steven Frank wrote a book called *Speed Reading Secrets*. I highly recommend the read, even though this book represents an updated and more extensive version of it. Relevant to reading five or more words together at a time, he has an excellent exercise for developing that method for yourself. Placing three columns of words on the page, he prompts his reader to follow only the middle bolded words and see how many of the other words they can take in, even though the eyes of the reader are naturally drawn to the bolded words.

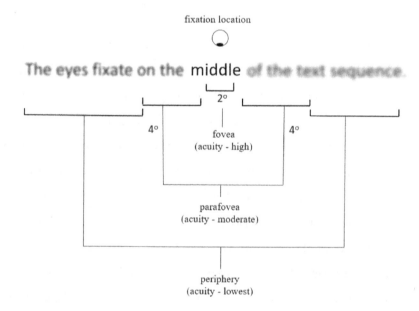

uncle	**penguin**	textbook
school	**light bulb**	jogging
alligator	**airplane**	adventure
umbrella	**soup**	fourteen
symbol	**friend**	bridge
literature	**envelope**	birthday
hungry	**skiing**	tennis
holiday	**shiny**	mathematics
bedroom	**clouds**	degree
green	**pencil**	nighttime
computer	**shoes**	dinner
graduation	**peanut**	candles
calendar	**elevator**	skate
ocean	**wallet**	hearing
sunshine	**brave**	music
mittens	**feather**	sister
history	**title**	doorway
words	**subway**	shampoo
prism	**movies**	occupation
sidewalk	**stomach**	princess

He then instructs his reader to try it again without the bolded words, just following the center column downward. The goal is to concentrate on just the middle section and see how many words the reader picks up anyway. Without the bolded word to take away the focus of your eye, your brain will process more words as your eye wanders more.

happiness	database	brakes
postage	capital	December
quantity	telephone	wristwatch

Boston	freedom	stapler
panther	pizza	motive
earthquake	socks	newspaper
maple	combination	squash
medicines	shoehorn	antenna
inflation	hammer	clothing
Spanish	detective	spectacle
knot	armchair	banister
postcard	temperature	modem
sticker	catalog	lawyer
bookstore	goggles	island
laundry	telephone	alarm
Monday	elevator	service
village	badge	guarantee
waterfall	note	evening
photograph	concert	plumber
ticket	locomotive	bubble
siren	octopus	professor

The relatively simple exercise demonstrates how easy this tactic can be. Frank points out that this technique translates even better to full sentences since they seek to convey a complete idea and the words flow together much better in that form. The words next to each other are not random, with no connection to each other. You do not actually need to read every word to get the idea of the sentence. As a final case and point, he puts a third column of words.

Once	you	train
your	eye	to
read	this	new

way,	you	find
that	it	is
not	so	difficult
to	do.	

Clark points out that sometimes one can divide sentences into clauses that match up nicely and can be used to read in groups. For instance, "before eating breakfast, he went jogging". Not all sentences are that conveniently cut up, though, and clauses vary in length. Some sentences get disjointed due to variation in word length. Dividing words and sentences on the page is still possible, though, just with diligent and somewhat creative application. Using the "Gettysburg Address" as an example text, he shows how you can divide it into columns that work better, with three or four words per column.

Four score and	seven years ago	our fathers brought
		forth conceived in
		Liberty,
on this continent	a new nation,	that all men
dedicated	to the proposition	
are created equal.		

Now we are engaged	in a great civil war,	testing whether that
		nation, and so
		dedicated,
or any nation	so conceived	on a great battle-field
can long endure.	We are met	to dedicate a portion
of that war.	We have come	for those who here
of that field,	as a final resting place	might live.

gave their lives	that this nation	that we should
It is altogether fitting	fitting and proper	
do this.		

Ron Cole advocates for this style of reading as well, grouping two, three, four, and five words together to develop and practice this skill. In his book, *SuperReading for Success*, he outlines an innovative and unique reading method that he calls the Eye-Hop. He claims that simply more utilization of this method will correlate to an increase in the reading effectiveness score of the subjects. His methods align similarly to the example from the book written by Steven Frank, but differ in that Cole focuses more on the words themselves than the columns they fall into. He constructs only two columns of words in his book, and the first set involves only pairs of words. A brief excerpt about Basic Astronomy primes the brain of the reader for what follows shortly after it. The three word eye-hop details explorations of Ernest Shackleton and other famous explorers to the South Pole. The four word eye-hop tells the story of The Optimist and further challenges the brain to group words together. At this point, Cole predicts that most of his readers will experience 'the breakthrough', without pronunciation, grasping the full meaning of the phrase. If it does not happen at the four word level, Cole guarantees it will at the five word eye-hop, given the logistical challenge of pronouncing each of the five words in half a second. Therein lies the goal of the Ron Cole eye-hop. On top of ensuring the processing of five words at a time, Cole forecasts a 75 percent recollection of the content in a general, gist-of-it way, not necessarily word for word. He encourages reading as quickly as possible while maintaining at least that level of comprehension.

Follow the Text with a Guide

If this lengthy digression and topic does not work for you, I have good news, there is another useful method. Meta-guiding has been around for some time and can help you accomplish this goal of reading five or more words at a time. It sets the pace for your eye by guiding it to certain words using a pen, pencil, or your finger. By tracking your eye and standardizing the amount of time you spend on each word, you can keep your eye moving along the page. There is a reason that children use the technique when they learn how to read. It helps to move from one word to the next while boosting reading speed and retention. Albeit for different purposes, adults can benefit from it too. The difference is that adults use it much faster, and that is where the trick lies. Working your way up, the faster you can move your finger across the page and follow it with your eyes, the quicker you can read. Acting as a tracker for your eyes, it sets the pace for your eyes and helps you focus from word to word.

Jordan Harry, notable entrepreneur of StudyFast, talks about this exact issue and how, if you fixate too often on each line, you will not only slow down your reading, but tire your eyes as well. Familiarity mitigates this phenomenon, he says, increasing the efficiency of your eye movements and allowing for an increase in reading speed. Part of that increase in efficiency depends on your ability to co-opt your peripheral vision for reading purposes. Doing so, according to Harry, will reduce the number of fixations required per line to about three. By processing more information at one time, it should enhance the quality of the bigger picture of the information without sacrificing understanding. Regular work and addressing of these points should enable you to read quicker.

Harry may just be the poster-child for speed reading since he is just 20 years old and has expanded Study Fast to 15,000 people in 147 countries. Overcoming a speech impediment, he now boasts a reading speed of 1,500 words per minute, the same speed this book promises. He offers everything from Online Courses to workshops to events and speaking engagements. Truly impressive, considering his age and childhood condition.

Jim Kwik espouses meta-guiding as well for biological and developmental reasons. He cites that children do it on their own until they are taught to not rely on it. You do it subconsciously when you count things or need extra focus on what you read. From an evolutionary standpoint, your eyes are pretuned to pick up on motion, essential for hunting and survival skills developed by our ancestors. Visual pacing improves focus by pulling our attention through the information rather than segmenting it. He also notes the inherent connection between sight and touch, similar to that of smell and taste. Smell is a large portion of taste, for evidence just eat anything when you have a cold. Your food simply does not taste as good. He quotes many people saying that they feel more tuned into their reading when they use a visual pacer. Perhaps the biggest point toward this connection, though, is the development of Braille, reading designed for those who are blind. Their sense of touch effectively becomes their sense of sight and the entire mechanism by which they read.

For those looking for a simple meta-guiding technique, stick with tracing each line with a pen, pencil, or your finger. If you, however, seek something more advanced than that, here is a preview of coming attractions. In Chapter ten: Learn Faster With Advanced Learning

Techniques, you will find the complicated hand motions developed by Evelyn Wood that released with her groundbreaking speed reading guide in 1959. Considered among the first documented speed reading specialists, she outlines several unique motions one can adopt to speed read, helping your eyes take in the words on the page faster. Stay tuned and read until the end for that, if for no reason other than curiosity.

Leverage Apps to Improve Your Reading

Rapid Serial Visual Presentation often gets used by apps that help with reading speed. By showing single words on the screen in front of you, this method removes the need for your eyes to move. This greatly decreases the time you need to process the information, much like the example MIT image processing experiment. As you get used to the system, the app will naturally increase the speed at which it shows you words, theoretically boosting your reading speed. The speed that words come up can surprise you, so much so that you do not realize that you understand them. However, the downside of this, given the sheer amount of words you see, your working memory gets overloaded. The words come faster than you can deal with them, and you skip some or simply do not process them.

If you decide that apps are the way to go, BookRiot has a list of apps that lend themselves to shrinking your TBR, or To Be Read. They are as follows; "Spreeder", "Reedy", "Read Me!", "Speed Reading", "Speed Reader", "Quick Reader", "Focus-Speed Reader", "Seven Speed Reading App", "Outread", and "Acereader iPad". Their compatible operating systems vary, some only on iOS, some only on Android, and a couple for desktop and browsers. Some are free, while others cost money in their respective app store. The range is far and wide, and I would be very willing to bet there is an app for your appetite, regardless of what your parameters are. If one works for you, download it and start using them to read! Keep in mind, new apps develop each day just as old apps leave the market, so some of these apps may be gone or replaced by the time you read this.

Another app that BookRiot does not mention but that a *MindTools* article does is "Spritz". Using similar RSVP, it released to much acclaim in 2014, even garnering an article in CNN Business that detailed the reactions people made to it, some awed, and some nauseated. Without beating a dead horse, the RSVP has skeptics, especially as one of many RSVP apps on the market, including at the time "Velocity". A minor difference, having one character in red as a focal point, leads to claims that "Spritz" more effectively capitalizes on RSVP while maintaining retention because the one-colored letter makes it easier to follow. The claim has some scientific backing, according to *Medical Daily*, as the brain takes 80 percent of its time locating the optimal recognition point for a given word and 20 percent actually reading it. That being said, speed reading expert Scott Young calls it improbable, considering that the brain can only grasp a 3-5 word "chunk" of information at once. He says our mental RAM just cannot sustain the levels of stimulation that "Spritz" utilizes. He also calls out "Spritz" for claiming research backs the application, but was unable to find any credible, independent, peer-reviewed research to support the claims. All of these apps share a commonality. You can supposedly read at 1,000 words per minute, but you risk comprehension loss and nauseation. The verdict: RSVP technology is not what it is cracked up to be.

A 2000 conference paper published by the University of Manchester in England concluded this very tradeoff. It admitted its value as a technique to facilitate information browsing and search but that it involves a drop off in comprehension. The human visual information processing system limits its use, and at the time, the paper added that much remains to be understood before wide and robust employment in practical applications.

Avoid Regression with Improved Focus

All of these practices, particularly the effective ones, assume that you don't pause or regress during your reading. Getting to the end of a page or halfway through an article and realizing that you have not taken in what you read usually forces you to go back and reread it. Similarly, coming across a word you cannot remember forces you to stop and regress to the technique you used as a child. Reread it for context and to try to understand what it means. With more difficult readings, this happens more frequently.

Jordan Harry, the aforementioned entrepreneur and champion of the effectiveness of speed reading, blames a lapse in concentration rather than a lack of understanding. Distractions cause this more than anything else, even when we think we have been diligently reading. Whether it is a comment by someone sitting in the same room, a text on your phone, or an errant thought, we often get distracted much easier and more frequently than we like to admit.

How do you change this? You can start by reigniting your interest in whatever you are reading. "When our brain wanders, it is because we

49

have become passive. We need to be curious," says Harry. Get actively inquisitive — tap into your inner kid, the one who demands, "But what does that mean?" and "Who is that?" Other questions recommended by Harry are "What am I looking for?" and "What key words and figures do I need to find?" You might also check in every few minutes and simply ask yourself, "What have I learned so far?"

Don't Fixate

In addition to regression, the other bad habit to avoid is fixation. This happens when our eyes catch on a word or a phrase we read on a page. Often going hand in hand with regression, fixation causes us to linger on random spots, impeding our speed. Rather than going back and reading again, fixation freezes us as we think through what a word or phrase means. Harry refers anyone who will listen back to meta-guiding. A tool we use while we read, it helps maintain our reading speed, he says. Often we do not realize that we are reading too fast or slow until it is too late, and we have lost retention or speed. Harry also praises it for forcing our eyes to read faster.

Another bad habit to pay attention to when reading faster is reading out of control. What does that mean? Well, reading out of control entails not purposely reading at a certain speed. This can work both in the faster and slower direction. When you get swept up in a book and turn the pages faster and faster because you are enthralled in the text, that is reading out of control. When your reading grinds to a screeching halt and you labor through every sentence to try to keep everything straight, that is also reading out of control. Part of this is natural since some writing naturally reads faster or slower. The trick here is to try to moderate the reading speed, maintaining a balance between speed and moderation where the text calls for it. An article on the website *Develop Good Habits* debunks the misconception that speed is the emphasis of speed reading and encourages this focus on control. The speed aspect controls one part of how we read and is a supplemental ability, not the essence of speed reading.

Overlook Unimportant Words

That same article, "How to Read Faster: 9 Steps to Increase your Speed in 2020", offers much of the same advice we've seen: decreasing subvocalization, establishing a baseline, meta-guiding, minimizing eye movement, skimming and scanning, and a commitment to practicing and evaluating your speed. However, it offers an interesting and seemingly overlooked piece of advice. Skip small, unimportant words. Based on the premise that saving an extra thirty seconds per page equates to an entire hour and a half in the longer run, the article suggests overlooking small words such as articles and prepositions. You know, words that would benefit you much more in a game of Scrabble. The logic is that their contribution to the overall text is minimal at best. In rare cases when they are necessary, the context of the sentence generally fills in the blank for you. For instance, take that last sentence and remove the small words: in, the, of, the, in, the, for. A decrease from 19 words to 12 does not seem very significant, but when every sentence is cut almost in half, it matters. You can get through each sentence about twice as fast and retain the essence of what it conveys.

If for some reason that train of thought does not work for you, flip it on its head. Rather than eliminating the less useful words, focus on finding the key words in a reading. Returning to basic grammar for a moment, find the subject and verb of the sentence. There is almost always more to a sentence than just those components unless taking, for example, the simple sentence about 'I ran', for instance. Identifying these parts, though, will give you important clues. Reading a sentence that begins 'the author demonstrated' will help your eyes look for the crucial third part of a sentence, the object. What is the author demonstrating? Recognizing the three building blocks of a sentence will help you process the sentence faster and allow you to focus on the substance of it. If you like, further grammatical analysis can help you decipher between dependent and independent clauses, allowing you to get to the point of a sentence quicker.

Even without any grammatical knowledge or assessment of a sentence, you can do as Abby Marks Beale does and just look at words that serve more than providing sentence structure. She gives a paragraph to her reader and tells them to read it as usual. Then she instructs them to just read the bolded words. Your eye will naturally focus on them, but not at the full expense of the other, less important words. You still see them, she says, but you do not read them, starting the process to expand your peripheral vision. Here is the paragraph I mentioned, for your benefit.

"The **best way** to **achieve** this is to **read key words** and/or **phrases. Key words** are the **bigger, more important words** in a **sentence, just like** the **headlines** of a **newspaper provide** the **essence** of the **content. Learning** to **stop** your **eyes** on the **words** that are **typically three letters** in **length** or **longer** and

those which carry the **most meaning** of a **sentence** are **keywords.**"

Beale offers an alternative to this as well. Rather than picking out words, she suggests to pick out groups of them that form a thought. She provides another paragraph that contains two sentences with slash marks dividing thoughts. She urges her reader to go through the paragraph, ignoring the slashes the first time and using them the second. This method and the aforementioned constitute active reading methods that require focus on behalf of the reader to what they read and how their eyes move across a given page. Here is the second example, again for your benefit.

"Additionally, sentences contain groups of words/ that form a thought./ Looking for these thought groups/ encourages a wider visual swath/ while gaining higher understanding/ of the material."

As with anything, these techniques take time to learn. With proper dedication and practice, though, you can adopt them and use them for yourself quickly enough. It is a matter of conditioning your eyes and brain to act in certain ways and respond to certain stimuli.

Chapter Summary

- Before you start reading, set a goal and keep it in mind as you read. Doing so reminds you why you are reading and helps you look for words and phrases that will further your goal.

- Skimming aids this practice, as it can help you gloss over less important sections. It can also give you a preview of what you are reading.

- When skimming, subvocalization becomes an impediment to reading faster. But rather than focusing on stopping it, try to form a new habit to replace it.

- Read groups of words instead of individual ones. By taking in three, four, five, or however many words at a time, you can cut down on the amount of time you spend on each word.

- There are several tactics to help you develop this skill. Steven Frank sets up simplistic columns for you to train your eyes to follow only the middle column, while still being able to read the left and right ones.

- Ron Cole accomplished a similar goal with his trademarked eye-hop, progressing from the first word to the second, then the third, the fourth, and the fifth. He claims that his readers will experience a breakthrough at either the fourth or fifth eye-hop, since in the half a second your eye takes to jumps from the first to the last word, your brain simply cannot pronounce every word in between. Nonetheless, you still get the gist of the grouping of words.

- Meta-guiding tracks your eye movement across the page and moderates your reading by standardizing the pace. Use your finger, a pen, a pencil, or something else to lead your eye.

- Experts love this technique, particularly young phenom Jordan Harry, who by the age of 20 became an entrepreneur and developed StudyFast, a United Kingdom based company, of which he is the Chief Executive Officer. StudyFast takes the basic principles of speed reading and adapts them so that their nearly 15,000 customers in 147 countries can, well, study faster.

- Meta-guiding can consider Jim Kwik solidly in its corner as well, as he heralds the effectiveness because it is a natural thing we do. Children do it, you do it when you do not realize it, and it is a biological instinct to hyper focus on movement from our days as hunter and prey. He also notes the inherent connection between sight and touch, similar to taste and smell, and uses the Braille reading system as an example. Expanding your awareness of all that goes into reading, he also lists things that will help, beginning with checking your eyes and wearing any reading glasses you may have. Among the other recommendations, keep your surroundings cold to sharpen your focus, keep them positive with anchors to encourage your subconscious, read in natural light when possible, listen to music around the speed of a natural heartbeat of 60 beats per minute, practice good posture, with your body and the book, stay hydrated, and use your whole brain.

- Rapid Serial Visual Presentation (RSVP) usually comes with the latest speed reading software or app. By placing words one at a time in one location on the screen, it removes the need for your eyes to move across the page and can boost your reading speed. It can result in working memory overload, though, and inhibit retention.

- RSVP technology is one of those fad trends that took off at various points in the 2010s, and there are dozens of them out there, each a little different and claiming to be the silver bullet in speed reading. They are as follows: Spreeder, Reedy, Read

Me!, Speed Reading, Speed Reader, Quick Reader, Focus-Speed Reader, Seven Speed Reading App, Outread, and Acereader iPad. They can help you get reading faster, but it is kind of cheating, since it is first and foremost not a practical text, and second, you only see one word at a time.

- Like every how-to guide, there are things to avoid as well. Regression is when you go back and reread what you just should have, seriously slowing down your reading. It comes from a lapse of concentration, according to Jordan Harry. His remedy? Renew your interest in what you are reading. Piquing your curiosity helps mitigate distractions and prevents passive reading.

- Fixation can also halt your reading, as your eye pauses on certain words or phrases. Harry recommends meta-guiding to keep your eyes moving.

- Focus on controlling your speed, not letting yourself go too fast or slow down too much. The average speed is essential to speed reading. It is no real use to read certain sections at 1,000 words per minute when the next one drops to 200 words per minute. That drops your average significantly to 600 words per minute, a fast reading speed but not the goal you may have set.

- Skip unimportant words to help you breeze through sentences. Some words are technically necessary but do not really contribute much to a sentence, especially when context more than suffices. Small words like if, is, so, the, to, and others only get in the way of your efforts to save time. It is a different skill and takes time to develop, but can assist you in your goal of reading faster.

- Conversely, focus on key words to facilitate your understanding. Often, it is easier to do something positive rather than eliminate something negative.

- Additionally, you can consolidate parts of sentences into thoughts to break the sentence into fewer parts that you need to understand, utilizing the capability of your eye to take in multiple words at once.

- If you just hate grammar, Abby Marks Beale has a method for picking up the important words on their own. Focus on reading words three letters or longer and move between them as quickly as you can. She also suggests grouping words into singular thoughts. These four, five, or however many word clusters can be processed as one and naturally go together, so she says they ease the ability to understand sentences in smaller parts.

These tips help improve the speed at which you read. The next chapter will give you complementary skills to better assist you in reading comprehension. Because what is the use of reading quickly if you do not understand it? Anyone can flip through pages quickly. A true master will almost completely comprehend what he or she reads on top of it.

CHAPTER SIX:

Reading Comprehension

Have you ever mindlessly flipped through the pages of a book that you really do not want to read? Maybe a textbook or assigned reading? Well, that is effectively what you do when you attempt to speed read without an accompanying focus on comprehension. There is a considerable difference between reading at high speeds mechanically for the sake of doing so and understanding what you read. Equally so, there is a difference between reading a text and comprehending it. When speed reading, your goal should not be to get through it as quickly as you can, particularly if you are learning a new skill. It is important that you understand the text you consume, particularly if you strive toward knowledge acquisition.

This may sound odd or counter-intuitive, but a tactic that helps with reading comprehension is to do more than just read the words on the page. Visualize what you read. There is such a thing as visualization and dynamic comprehension, meaning that as you read, you form visual pictures, instead of repeating the words within your mind, or 'listening' to yourself mentally. If you can manage to do this, it makes your reading more efficient. If you happen to be reading a story, you seem to be 'inside' the story. If you are absorbing facts, for instance about a new mechanical device, your reading will actually enable you to visualize just how that device works. Visualization forms the basis of the human condition. This makes sight a crucial function and tool for us to use to our advantage.

On the other hand, we learn to use language as a tool, making it somewhat unnatural to human development. It takes a conscious and deliberate effort to incorporate language into our quiver of skills as human beings. Different groups of people from different locations around the world developed language as a series of signs and symbols to communicate or record. These signs, symbols, and sounds have an arbitrary relationship with their meanings, which is why there are so many different languages. It's this arbitrary nature that makes languages difficult to learn, even if we have an innate capacity to learn them as an imperative to communicate. We are constantly translating to understand language.

In order to comprehend effectively while speed reading, you need to similarly 'translate' the language of words to the language of the mind, which is visualization. If you can adapt this somewhat abstract process to your reading practices, you will find that your reading comprehension can increase by a factor of 30% or more. So by bringing the mechanical aspect of reading 'up to speed' with that of the human mind, you can maximize both reading and comprehension. You will find your reading speed easily tripled and remember everything that you read effectively as well.

This seems like a particularly lofty goal. Can you really get to the point where you read upwards of 900 words per minute and still retain every last one? Do not let trying to retain everything phase you. If you are trying to memorize the entire book, you probably will not succeed. While some people take speed-reading to an extreme, there are others who TRY to take retention to an extreme. Unless you have an eidetic memory, also known as photographic memory, you will fail, even if by the slimmest of margins. More likely than not, you will get frustrated and contemplate giving up because you did not fully maximize your time and reading. Rather than shooting for a full and complete picture of what you read, when you read for knowledge acquisition you do so to form mental models in your mind. A mental model is essentially someone's world view of a certain concept, whether it works and aligns with physical reality or not. So when you read, you either develop an understanding for a new concept or you correct your understanding of an old concept, making your previous perspective more nuanced and complicated. As you get through more books, you will notice that authors are often redundant. In fact, several books will have the same overlapping information. Authors from the same category will often reference or quote each other. All this redundancy will drill the information into your head and automatically solve your retention issues. So simply focus on getting through more books and never stop.

Not knowing the meaning of a word can slow down your reading, making efforts to get through your reading quickly even more difficult. One of the secrets to overcoming this may seem obvious but takes a concerted effort to attain. Expanding your vocabulary will widen the range of words you can understand easily, but this takes the diligence to incorporate new words into daily use. The wider your vocabulary, the less you have to pause and look up the meanings of unknown words. Learn the meanings of new words when you have spare time. It will boost both your reading skills and your overall intelligence. In the same way you set a goal for your speed reading, you could set a goal to learn a certain amount of words per day or week. Before long, if you add three new words per day to your vocabulary, for instance, you will find your repertoire of words greatly expanded. There are plenty of excellent methods to learn a new word per day. I, for instance, use the Word Genius Word of the Day email blast. If you find two or three or however many more you like, use them to supplement each other and increase your vocabulary by the day. In conjunction with that, you will find fewer and fewer words you do not recognize in your reading, automatically increasing your reading speed.

A trick less for your overall reading speed and more for boosting retention when you read, play the "recall" game. At the end of each page in a book or the end of a few paragraphs in an article, pause and recall what you just read. Write a few key words in the margin to summarize what you just read. This will help for a couple of reasons. First, you ingest the information on the page again. This mindful act of retention will increase your understanding almost automatically. Second, putting the information into your own words demonstrates an understanding of the information and represents some level of mastery of it. Each of these techniques constitutes an aspect of active reading. By doing things such as recalling, pausing, or taking notes rather than passively taking in information, you keep engaged with what you read.

Maybe the most important consideration and factor in reading comprehension is the environment you are trying to read in. Are you in a quiet place where you can focus? Or are you somewhere loud and noisy, with more distractions than you can deal with? There is a reason why libraries are so quiet and librarians enforce it so fiercely. It is just easier to stay focused and not get distracted when there is not much going on around you. One concession I will make, though, is that in a quiet environment, each sound and distraction gets amplified. A sneeze or bump against a bookcase, or whatever the source may be, can be heard by everyone and induces the stare of shame from anyone who can see you. Still, though, fewer distractions are easier to ignore. Compared to a coffee shop or your morning commute on the train or bus, a library is a sanctuary of silence. That is not to say it is impossible to focus when you find yourself in such an environment, but it is substantially harder. You require much more discipline and conditioning to keep from getting distracted. Be mindful of where you are and what kind of person you are when it comes time to focus. Find an environment that works best for you, and read there as much as you can.

Just as much as limiting the external distractions that you cannot necessarily control, eliminate those that you have full control over. Some people enjoy reading with some sort of background noise, like music or ambient noise. This can help, without a doubt, giving you something to intentionally block out, if that is how you choose to think about it. If this works for you, I encourage you to try it or adopt it. However, be mindful of the impact whatever device that plays this noise has on your productivity. Our devices, smartphones, tablets, computers, and so on and so forth, have so much functionality in this day and age. Odds are, whatever you use to play music or ambient noise will have some sort of notification buzzing or chiming to demand your attention. I do understand that sometimes you have to be connected in order to get important updates, but as much as you can, try to silence or ignore these pesky little interruptions. Dedicate time solely to reading and block out the noises of our digitally interconnected world for a time. Not only will it help you focus, it will provide some meditative time, as you quiet your brain from the constant stimulation. You may find yourself reading for that purpose just as much as the sake of reading. You will notice too that you can comprehend more when you make a concerted effort to focus on your reading.

More than anything, challenging your reading comprehension strengthens it just like any exercise designed to test and grow a certain muscle. This is true whether your concentration is speed or whether it is comprehension. You are more than allowed to read at reduced speeds if you want to tackle a difficult or new reading. In fact, I would encourage that from time to time. That way, when you go to speed read something similar or related, you can do so while sacrificing less retention. Challenging your reading comprehension will not directly help your speed reading, but it will help your overall reading and ability to recall information when you do apply speed reading techniques.

Chapter Summary

- There is a difference between reading quickly to speed through a text and reading quickly while also focusing on retention.
- Visualization can help with retention by constructing a broader perspective of the information and tuning into our visual nature.
- Do not try to retain everything. Even the best speed readers, or readers in general, cannot remember the entirety of what they read. Rather, they retain a percentage of it, between 60 and 85 percent for the most skilled speed readers. Instead, they form

working mental models, which will enhance previous understandings or develop new ones.

- Expand your vocabulary to reduce the number of words you do not know when you read.

- Play the 'recall' game. Every so often within a text, pause and remember what you read. If you are so inclined, leave a note in the margin. Active reading in this way promotes a greater understanding of what you read as you process the information more times.

- Where you read matters tremendously. Think about yourself and your attention span. Try to read in an environment that suits your characteristics and matches your goals for reading.

- Challenge your reading comprehension when you can, at both high speeds and normal speeds. Reading with the intention of getting more out of it will help your speed reading, even though it will not necessarily increase your reading speed. Building your foundational reading comprehension makes retention when speed reading easier to accomplish.

This chapter should have helped you on your way to greater reading comprehension. In the following one, you will learn why you should use some of your free time to read, particularly if you find it laborious. After all, the more you read, the better you will get at it, particularly if you are reading actively and mindfully. Especially so if you are working on increasing your reading speed.

CHAPTER SEVEN:

Reading More in Your Free Time to Read Faster

Some people take to things much easier than others. Otherwise, we would all tryout for professional sports teams or symphony orchestras, or maybe write the next great novel. The reality, however, is that certain people are naturally better at some things than others, which is why you will never see me trying to guard Lebron James as he muscles his way toward the basket. It would take a tremendous amount of effort just to look even a little less helpless in that scenario, even if I wanted to do it. Similarly, if you find reading effortful, you would naturally want to do less of it. However, if you want to read more, you need to spend more time reading books which you like and find interesting. There is even more to it than that, though. Picking works that are easy to comprehend so prevents you from burning out quickly. This is, at least, where you should begin. Remember, challenging your own comprehension can improve your retention during speed reading. Nonetheless, there is a reason that people suggest reading books intended for children to help learn a new language. They read quickly, take little effort to follow, and contain words you probably already know, even if in another language. For those same reasons, minus the translation, you can start with quick reads like Harry Potter to boost your confidence and enjoyment in reading.

Stephen Krashen, highly relevant as a pioneer in second-language acquisition methods, conducted extensive research as a linguist about the various forms in which people learn new languages. He spearheaded a shift from previous rule-focused approaches to meaning-focused ones, particularly communicative language teaching, which is now the most widely accepted approach. In addition, he developed a controversial, but well-known, input hypothesis for language learning. This hypothesis argues that, when learning a new language, you need to accept high volumes of input at a comprehensible level. The application to regular reading, rather than with the goal of acquiring new language skills, lies in that if you understand less than 95% of the text, it will be too difficult to sustain your motivation to keep reading. When you think about it, this makes perfect sense. Struggling to understand something keeps you from enjoying reading it, and can frustrate or dissuade you from continuing. If you need a concrete example, recall a particularly convoluted book you may have read in English class and the themes, motifs, and character development your teacher smartly pointed out that you just plain missed. Or maybe you picked up an article from a high-brow publication and got lost in the nuance of some particular topic about which you know very little.

Again, this seems much easier said than done. Acknowledge that intention and action are two very different things, and one does not constitute the other. Sometimes intent does not turn into action. Sometimes it is because of lack of motivation, others because of lack of know-how. There is not much I can do about the former, but to help the latter, here are some suggestions for reading more:

Focus on building the habit. Reading is a skill — and skills take time to develop, they do not just appear overnight. When you just start out, you want to think about establishing the habit before anything else. Keep your expectations realistic, and keep yourself from getting too far ahead of yourself. Base your expectations on where you are, not necessarily where you hope to be, and set goals without making them unachievable. If you set unrealistic goals, you are going to crash and burn. If you fail to meet the goal, then you will feel discouraged and risk breaking the habit before you can really establish it. So focus on building the habit first. Tell yourself you are going to read for one hour a day no matter what. Or if that feels like it is too ambitious for you, start at fifteen minutes a day. Either way, work your way up to your target reading time. Meeting more little goals rather than fewer big ones may not give you as much momentary satisfaction, but will slowly but surely grow your confidence and abilities. Once you build some momentum, you will notice yourself get faster.

Reduce the barrier to entry. As human beings, we have mastered the art of procrastination, which may sound strange considering procrastination is doing nothing and putting off what you should be doing. We will come up with reason after reason to avoid doing something, even when we know better. To combat this, we need to eliminate resistance. One way to do this is to make "starting" the activity easier. Make reading so easy that it becomes almost unavoidable. Develop routines that lead you to read. You could read for however long when you get home at the end of the day since reading can relax your brain. Incentivize your reading somehow or another. Is there a particular activity you like to do or thing you like to have at a point in the day? Maybe you like to watch TV at night or eat dessert after dinner? Reading beforehand could give you an extra bit of satisfaction, tying them even closer to reading. Also, if you feel your TV watching gets in the way of your reading, doing so before would significantly reduce your guilt in watching TV rather than reading. If routines or incentivization do not work for you, you can keep a spare book or kindle in your bathroom or somewhere else that would turn idle time into potential reading time. This way, you can get at least 5–10 minutes of reading every morning. Another trick is to keep the book you want to read on the couch — opened to the current page you are on. You would have to actively choose not to read, picking up the book and moving it when all it would take to start reading would be to literally pick it up. If there is a smaller barrier to entry than that, I cannot think of it.

That is if the book you choose to pick up is one you're reading for pleasure. Have books that you genuinely want to read, which will encourage you to put in the time to read it. Think about what interests you most. Maybe there are certain individuals you admire or follow in the public realm. Picking up their autobiography, if they have one, could encourage you to read it. A book about their life could make you turn the pages as you learn more about their childhood, upbringing, education, and maybe a secret or two to their success. Are there certain things you have always wondered about but never really looked into? I guarantee you there is a book on it, if you look hard enough. Use your reading as a way to quench your curiosity, and make it a pleasurable thing to do.

If you find yourself in the middle of a book you do not like, switch books if you have to. Do not be afraid to leave a book unfinished and to switch books mid-reading. You do not have to commit to finishing every book you read. After all, life is too short to finish a bad book, and luckily you get to decide what constitutes a bad book. If you tend to get bored with one book or another, you can have around 3 to 5 books in your active pile of books you are currently reading. There is no universal rule that states that you have to read one book at a time, start to finish. You can have a book for any number of moods or mindsets you may be in. If you find yourself struggling to get through a certain hard book, switch to something you enjoy more, which may actually lead you to more important books down the line as you practice reading more.

Before you bite off more than you can chew with particularly difficult books, build up to harder books. If there is a really difficult book you want to read, start by reading more accessible commentaries, or related books that will make you familiar with the topic, ideas, and vocabulary. Research the book and the author to try to get a sense of the kind of language he or she uses when they write. This will give you some background knowledge which will make reading the harder book easier. Content knowledge is a big part of reading more fluently and efficiently, so if you struggle when you read a book, it might simply mean you need more background knowledge to process it properly. When you pick books that you want to read, the most important thing is that they are at the right level for you. It may have been considered cheating in school, but when you are reading for yourself there is absolutely nothing wrong with looking up Sparknotes, or any other summary or synopsis to help you keep track of what you are reading. This way you go into it with an idea and expectation of what you will read.

Build your foundation first. If you are having a particularly hard time with reading a book, spend the time to look up all the words you do not understand, search the concepts on Wikipedia or google around for the stories behind names and characters you do not recognize. This will initially take more time, but it will eventually help you read the rest of the book much faster.

Chapter Summary

- Reading comes more naturally to some people, but that does not mean that not everyone can do it. The more you do something the better you will get at it, and reading is the same way.

- Krashen's input hypothesis states that if you understand less than 95% of a given text, you will find it more difficult to keep reading it. Pick books or readings that are easy to understand.

- Start small and focus on building the habit before you make ambitious goals.

- Reduce the barrier to entry by making it easier to start reading. Place books in places you can not ignore them or read things that really pique your interest.

- Reading for pleasure will make reading seem like less like a choice and more like something you enjoy doing. Pick topics or authors you like. This is not a high school English class where you have to read a book assigned to you. You have the power of choice in the matter.

- You do not have to read every book cover to cover. You can switch between them, or stop reading them whenever you want.

- Start small and build big. You should not start with difficult books off the bat. Start with ones you know you can read at the speed and comprehension you want, then try ones that are a little harder, before you get to the hardest one you want to read.
- Build your foundation by doing a little research before you start reading. Whether it is major plot points or an overview of an article. A little bit of legwork before you begin will help you in the longer run.

Reading more will present one small detail, though. It will make keeping track of your reading hard since you have more to keep track of, naturally. The next chapter will give you some insight into how you can do this effectively. Providing multiple tactics and strategies to do so, you can choose which one best suits you. Adapting any of these will further your goal to read faster and ensure that you keep doing so actively.

CHAPTER EIGHT:

Tracking Your Reading Progress

Reading more will certainly boost your confidence. Like I said earlier, though, it will only have a limited effect on your reading speed if you're not actively tracking your progress and trying to improve. In order to truly increase your reading speed as I promised, you need to get serious and diligent about your speed reading practice. This involves setting goals and tracking your progress.

Try to consistently read sections of the same word-count and time your results. Calculate your reading speed using the calculation found in chapter four. Slowly push yourself to get faster. Start with a goal in mind for how many pages or words you want to read per-minute, and work until you reach that goal. Developing reading skills is the key to mental and professional growth. But remember not to empty the joy from learning. Success and growth should also be fun. Taking enjoyment out leads to resentment, but having fun helps you learn quicker. Studies consistently show that we learn more and progress faster when we enjoy what we are doing. As such, here are some ways to track your reading progress and keep engaged.

Goodreads

Take advantage of Goodreads Bookshelves. If you love reading and you do not have a Goodreads account, you need to change that. Now! Goodreads is basically social media for books. You can discover new books, track what you are reading, what you have already read, and you can interact with others through book reviews, comments, groups, and more. I spend much more time than I should on Goodreads, and it is my favorite way to keep track of everything I have read or want to read.

Goodreads tracks your reading for you each year. You can set a goal, and every time you mark a book as read in that year, Goodreads will update your progress, so you have a constant reminder of where you stand on your reading goal. Goodreads also publishes a reading report for you each year, so you can see a cool graphic about your reading journey.

Trello

Create a Trello Board dedicated to reading. Trello is a productivity tool that can be used for so many things, from school to work to life in general. It can be used to track travel plans, organize ideas, coordinate household to-do lists; and, of course, track your reading. If you are interested in trying Trello, the online tool is completely free and very versatile.

Pinterest

Use Pinterest for similar goals. Not quite the same functionality as Trello, Pinterest offers a similar objective to Goodreads, but in a format closer to Trello with a board of pictures, ideas, and thoughts. Incorporating the social media aspect, you can look at the boards that other people post for inspiration and log what you have read or what you hope to read using pictures. There are some interesting and famous people on Pinterest. Use their accounts or books for inspiration when you need some.

Spreadsheets

Create a custom spreadsheet to log your reading. Whether you choose to keep your spreadsheet online (using something like Google Sheets) or offline in Microsoft Excel, spreadsheets are a great way to keep track of reading goals and all of the books you have read. Using Google Sheets, you can also share with your family so everyone can track their reading in one place. Spreadsheets are a great way to actually visualize your reading goals. You can use a spreadsheet reading log to track what you read each year, what you purchase, and how you are doing for each challenge. It will boost your confidence in your reading as you see the list expand, particularly if using it as a friendly competition between friends or family. Not only that, it will help you figure out what books you like, what books you do not, how long it takes you to get through them, and if you are particularly adept at spreadsheets, create charts, graphs, and tables about your reading. Paper reading logs would be just as helpful, but not quite as informative.

Pen and Paper

If you've got an aversion to technology, all of this can be accomplished with a pen and paper, whether in a planner or loose leaf. Planners usually offer some extra pages in the back, as well as extra space on each calendar or diary page, meaning that there are plenty of options for how to track your reading.

Or, if you find yourself struggling with any of these, or need something more physical in your life, make your bedside table your reading list. Keep the five or so books, or however many, it does not matter, you are either currently reading or want to read next to you on your bedside table. It can be difficult to keep track of a reading list, especially if it is a mental list. Even physical lists on paper or a screen can be hard to track.

Of course, none of this matters much if you don't maintain sight of your goals. As you read, make sure you log your pace. Log how much progress you make toward your current WPM goal.

Chapter Summary

- There are many different ways to track your reading progress. It matters less which you choose than that you do it.
- Some people are just wicked smart and can keep track of their reading in their head. That is not realistic for everyone.
- Goodreads is an excellent way to keep track of your reading, as a social media platform dedicated to books and reading. It has all the benefits of a book club without the intermittent meetings,

potentially annoying members, and having to read books chosen for you. It lets you document which books you read, rate them to show whether you liked them or not, and provides opportunities to interact with friends as well. It even gives recommendations.

- Trello can be a useful tool as well. This free and versatile application can be used for your reading as well as anything else needing organization in your life.

- Creating a spreadsheet to log your reading can enable friendly competition between those you share it with and help you visualize your overall reading better. Plus, if you are good, you can create actual visual representations of your reading in the form of charts, graphs, and tables.

- There is nothing wrong with good, old-fashioned paper. Get a planner or find space in your current one for reading logs or notes.

- If all else fails, use the pile of books you have somewhere as your reading list. It gives you a more tangible way to keep track of your progress. When it shrinks, you get encouraged, maybe to go out and get more books from the bookstore or your local library.

By this point in the book, you have been introduced to all the basics of speed reading. This will give you a solid start on your way to increasing your reading speed. Chapter nine dives deeper into the technique that most expert speed readers use. Skimming and scanning can be the two methods by which you can quickly and easily increase your reading speed the most.

CHAPTER NINE:

Skimming or Scanning

We've discussed skimming and scanning briefly, but it's such a useful tool that it deserves its own chapter. Unfortunately, skimming gets a bad reputation. Few people recognize it as a skill for reading and, rather, consider it quite the opposite of reading. Many consider skimming and scanning a tool to avoid reading, or simply a means of figuring out whether something is worth reading in full. This is just plain wrong. Skimming and scanning are not nearly that passive. In fact, as you will find in this chapter, both are difficult, intentional acts that require their own levels of mastery to do properly.

Skimming is a process of speed reading that involves visually searching the sentences of a page for clues to the main idea. It can mean reading the beginning and ending for summary information, then optionally the first sentence of each paragraph to quickly determine whether to seek still more detail, as determined by the questions or purpose of the reading. These sections are most important because they will tell you the most about what you read. The introduction gives you a preview of coming attractions for whatever the reading may be, giving you a chance to see what it is about and prepare you for what it is going to tell you. Similar to the introduction to the passage, the first sentence of a paragraph will generally tell you what the paragraph is about. It lays the foundation for the main points that follow or gives you an idea of what to expect. The conclusion will, assuming the author is good at doing so, wrap up the reading neatly as if in a bow. It should recap the main points in a succinct way. A well-written conclusion will tell you why you have spent your time well by reading everything that came before it. Lastly, it will leave you with something, hopeful resonant, that you have gained by reading.

Two techniques that involve looking only for the most relevant bits of information first will prime you for what is soon to come. Since you are already familiar with the main parts of the text, you will not be slowed down by confusing or surprising parts when you come to them in your reading. Keep in mind that, while skimming and scanning work best for non-fiction, it can be applied to fiction too. In a novel, skim the chapter for character development, key points of dialogue, and major plot points. Then read it at a faster pace than you normally would. Even though you are reading it twice, you are reading it faster, since you will have picked up the most important things on the first breeze through. Then, on the second read, you pick up more minute details that you missed on the initial skim. These two readings should be enough to parse any relevant information, but should you feel ambitious, a third go-around would be warranted, especially for more difficult books.

Okay, that sounds great! You say. But how do you do it? Here is a step by step process as to how to skim a text. Skimming — getting the essence from reading material without reading all the words — boils down to knowing what parts to read and what parts to pass by. Following are some tips and techniques for recognizing what is important to read in the act of skimming.

Know What You Want

Before you start skimming, ask yourself what you want to get from the text. Think of two or three terms that describe what you want to know, and, as you skim, keep an eye out for those two or three terms. Actively searching for them will help you find them easier than if you just passively read the text. Aimlessly skimming with no particular purpose is usually fruitless and boring. The lack of focus on an object leads to spacing out. I am sure you are familiar with this feeling. Skimming is not the same as passive reading, in fact, it is the opposite. Give your reading, and your skimming a purpose by looking out for keywords. Come into your reading armed with a couple of questions as well. Not only will they help you determine what you want to get out of the reading, if they go unanswered at the end, you have some fodder for more reading in the future.

Read Vertically

When skimming, you move your eyes vertically as much as you move your eyes horizontally. In other words, you move your eyes down the page as much as you move them from side to side. Skimming is a bit like running down stairs. Yes, you should take one step at a time, and running down stairs is reckless, but you also get there faster by running. And what happens when you walk only sideways down stairs? A whole lot of nothing. Nonetheless, this is still reading, not actually travelling down stairs. As such, to find what you're looking for, you've got to occasionally move your eyes left-to-right as well as up and down. This is both a caution against too much vertical reading and a reminder to move vertically as much as you can. Moving too quickly down the page will lessen the degree to which you understand each line. Not moving down fast enough will slow down your reading speed. It is a delicate balance.

Put Yourself in the Author's Shoes

Every article, book, and web page is written to make a point of some kind. Whether it is an academic article meant to present a certain hypothesis or a novel conveying a theme, everything has a point to it. Otherwise, it would not be worth the read. If you can detect the strategies that the author uses for making his or her point, you can separate the important from the unimportant material. Detecting the tendencies of the author requires you to put yourself in his or her place. Besides noticing the material on the page, notice how he or she presents the material. See whether you can recognize how the author places background material, secondary arguments, tangential information, and just plain frippery. Do the frills come before the point or the other way around? Does the author come right out and say it clearly or make you figure it out for yourself to some degree?

Another critical component of this is picking up on subtext that the author may have inserted, conveying ideas that are not explicitly stated. Some authors rely on their readers to make inferences and assumptions about the reading, particularly in literary or creative writing. This can often be just as important as the actual text. Many people think that a highly focused and sharp attention to detail can only pick up on subtext, but that is not true. Subtext can come in many forms from many techniques. The most important thing is paying attention to it and being able to interpret it the way the author wants you to. Additionally, interpreting the overall tone of the text, some believe, can get lost in reading too fast. Again, that is not true. Your brain still picks up punctuation at high speeds, and that is the key to unlocking the intonation that the author writes with. Lastly, be aware of the subject matter that the author writes about as much as possible and read with the big picture the author wants you to see in mind. This will improve reading comprehension dramatically. Determining the style of writing in this way can help you identify what's important.

Preread

If you are skimming for the purpose of knowledge acquisition, pre-read before you start skimming. For example, if reading an article, examine it before you read. By pre-reading an article before you skim, you can pinpoint the parts of the article that require your undivided attention and the parts that you can skip. It may seem counterintuitive since you then read it twice, but skipping the sections that do not pertain as much to your goal for reading cuts down pretty incredibly on time. *Speed Reading Lounge* offers four strategies to assist you in your skimming and scanning. Preview key sentences to pick up on one idea, perhaps the key idea, then practice honing in on the most interesting bits. Then scan names and numbers to get a narrative of the details about people, places and concepts. Identify trigger words to keep a lookout for important phrases and keywords. Use the pencil you may have for meta-guiding to jot them down. This will help ensure that you are getting what you want and need out of the reading. Lastly, read the title, including the headlines and subheadlines. In this world of search engine optimization, often the title will include key terms to look for throughout the reading, while subheadlines can give you an idea of the structure or anchor points in the text. Consider, for instance, this very book, Proven Speed Reading Techniques: Read More Than 300 pages in 60 minutes—A Guide for Beginners on How to Read Faster with Comprehension (Includes Advanced Learning Exercises). The title tells you what you will be reading and what you will get out of it, proven techniques for speed reading so you can read 300 pages in 60 minutes. The subheadline outlines the structure of the book, taking you from beginner status to reading faster while maintaining comprehension. Lastly, and more peripherally, it includes advanced learning exercises.

Pre-reading in this way will help you, as the article states, to differentiate which type of reading you will be doing, deciding whether to use speed reading or full comprehension modes. In a helpful analogy, author Mark Ways distinguishes between microwave and oven reading. Microwave readings refer to contents that include technical information, detailed explanations, guidelines or instructions. In this case, you care less about how it is written than the information included so that you can apply it in a real-world sense to your life. Oven reading compares closely to baking in this analogy and requires more time to heat and digest than microwave. Ways uses the example of biographies, success stories, or life experiences as things you would want to digest fully to better understand. Skimming and scanning will give you the main ideas but depth and diligence yield the most from this type of reading. Identifying which books you can skim and scan your way through will help you focus your reading and spend your time more wisely. Skimming or scanning a book that does not lend itself to those techniques will result in frustration more often than not, impeding your reading progress.

You may say, 'this seems a lot like just skimming to me, how is it different?' Well, pre-reading involves understanding the outline and construction of a text before you read it. For instance, you would glance over it without digging into the actual paragraphs. You would notice the chapter titles, subheadings, and then the chapter summary at the end. You would not engage this particular as a part of a pre-read. That's when the skimming comes into play. The different types of reading Mark Ways identified that are mentioned above can only be determined after a thorough pre-read. The purpose of it is to gain as much of an idea of the text before you skim it or scan it.

Read the First Sentence of Each Paragraph

The introductory sentence of each paragraph usually describes what follows in the paragraph. When you skim, read the first sentence in each paragraph and then decide whether the rest of the paragraph deserves a read. If it does not, move on. This works much better for non-fiction writing since fiction paragraphs do not follow the same constructs and can contain important plot or story enriching details in them. It would also be helpful to read the last sentence of the paragraph because it often succinctly summarizes the paragraph and segues into the next paragraph. The first and last sentences in a paragraph are often the most important ones. Sometimes you'll find it's completely unnecessary to read what's in between.

An article in the Journal of Experimental Psychology tested the effectiveness of skimming while reading. The authors conducted three experiments to determine this, using expository texts and only allowing for enough time for readers to get through half of each text. The first experiment found that skimming allows readers to obtain important ideas from each document at the expense of less important details. It also showed that they missed some inferences from the information included in the text. The second experiment determined that skimming and reading the first or second half of the paragraphs lead to the same amount of retention. This confirms what the paragraph above says, that skimming and reading the first sentence or so are both equally effective methods for speed reading. The study also found that due to the Website-like layout of the texts provided to the readers, skimming predicates on how pages link together, an indication of the ease of navigation through the document. Most interestingly, an analysis of reading times based on page and eye-tracking indicated that the text early on in the paragraphs, toward the beginning of a page, and at the front of the document received more attention from the readers. Again, this supports the assessment that skimming suffices when reading through a document under time pressure, according to the authors of the study.

Do not necessarily read complete sentences

The point of skimming is that you need not read every word on the page. If the start of a sentence holds no promise of the sentence giving you the information you want, skip to the next sentence. Read the start of sentences with an eye to whether they will yield useful information. For example, you do not need to read **this** entire sentence, or even the next few sentences, because it is just a pointless ramble about how if you had skipped the rest of it you would have saved yourself so much time and effort. It was not necessary at all, and when you take the sentence at its face value in the first few words, you do not get frustrated, especially when the sentences get long and convoluted and you start to question their grammatical correctness; and then they start to throw things in, like semicolons, which you have to harken back to English class to figure out if they are used right or not—that before you know it makes the sentence not worth your time. As a case in point, "For example, you do not need to read this entire sentence" took me less than a second to read. It took me about 11 to read the rest of it. In this case, the sentence literally told you that you do not have to keep reading, but there will not be many of them that do in your general reading. A better example may be: "The Stone Age was defined by an innovation in tools, as early humans began to incorporate things from the world around them to develop new ways to complete their tasks." The first part of the sentence, the independent clause, tells you the point of the sentence. The second part only serves to provide more information in the form of an example. Reading the first part but not the second gets you about as far as reading both.

Skip examples

There are some things you just don't have to read, much like the one I just provided. Authors often present examples to prove a point, but if you believe the point does not need proving, you can skip them. I could put an example here, but after that lengthy one, you would probably skip it anyway.

When skimming, do not be afraid to take a few more seconds and re-skim what you just read to ensure comprehension. You are already saving time by skimming rather than reading in-depth, so you would just save a little less by going backward for a short bit. You could also pre-skim, so you know a little of what to expect in what follows.

Chapter Summary

- Contrary to popular belief, skimming and scanning are active skills that do not rely on obtaining information through osmosis. That is to say, it is an active process that does not just happen on its own.

- Skimming prioritizes certain information at the expense of others. Scanning a text before you read it will help you identify which information will help you and which will not.

- Unproductive though it may seem, reading something twice in this manner, glancing over it then reading the parts you thought interesting quickly, will reduce your reading time because details don't bog you down.

- It works for both fiction and non-fiction writing. You have to identify different things in your first pass by, though. Whereas non-fiction is based on points helpful to the argument, fiction consists of plot points, dialogue, themes, or character development. You could skip things like descriptions, particularly wordy ones, for instance.

- Know what you want to read beforehand, going off of a title, headline, or something related that you have already read. It can be helpful to think of terms you want to learn or concepts you want to grasp better. Knowing what you're looking for always helps to find it.

- Read vertically. That is, do not move your eye so much side to side. Reading words in clusters will help with this. Careful not to move too far or fast vertically because you may miss information you want to read, which hopefully you have already identified.

- Think like the author. Much easier in non-fiction writing when there is a thesis you can identify but also practical in fiction, figure out what the point the author wants to prove. There is always at least one. More than that, try to figure out how they present it. Where is the evidence relative to the point?

- Preread. Evaluate the text. Big paragraphs or little ones? Are the sentences long or are they really short? Identify what you think will be the keywords and phrases. Come up with goals or questions you hope to fulfill by the end of the reading.

- Read the first sentence in each paragraph. Particularly in academic or scholarly texts, it may tell you all you need to know about the point the author makes in the paragraph. Read the last sentence too, it will often tell you what the paragraph said and lead you into the next one.

- Only read full sentences when the information serves you. When the information in the beginning piques your curiosity and makes you want to read more, do so. But do not keep reading sentences that do not give you much information, they only serve to bog you down and keep you from moving on to ones that actually fulfill the purpose you set for reading them.

- Skip examples. Particularly when they use phrases like, for example, for instance, as evidence, to demonstrate this, or anything else that can signify information that only supports the point. They can be harder to identify than that sometimes. You may just have to use your gut or intuition and skip the rest of the paragraphs at the risk of missing something important. Chances are, though, you will not miss too much. For instance, if you had only read 'skip examples', you probably would have gotten just as much out of this bullet point without reading my intentional rambling. It should show you what a sneaky, hiding example looks like, though. I hope you enjoyed this small, exemplary aside. You're welcome.

Congratulations! You have come to the end of basic speed reading. You can now go out into the world an intermediate speed reader and try these tips and tricks for yourself if you like. What was that? You want to know what the rest of the pages in this book are for? Since you asked, these are only for the daring. Chapter ten has more secret, advanced techniques that will help your speed reading even more. Okay, they are not so secret, but they are advanced. Read on to find out what they are. You are closer than you have ever been to becoming a master!

CHAPTER TEN:

Learn Faster with Advanced Techniques

Thank you for reading this far. In doing so you have demonstrated a desire to get the very most of this book. Some people see a chapter title like "Learn Faster with Advanced Techniques" and quit because they question whether or not it will be worth their time, or maybe they do not think they will be up to it. Or maybe they already got what they wanted out of the book, which is fine.

Here is your chance to get ahead of the pack. Gaining more knowledge has always been important for success. But the pace of modern life has become so quick that by the time you learn new facts they are already becoming outdated. So, we have to learn faster. And the most effective way to do that is to improve your reading speed and comprehension.

Metacognition

These advanced techniques require a careful look at your reading tendencies, analyzing them as much as possible to improve them. Metacognition is the first step to this end, as inaccessible as it may seem. In reality, simply thinking about how you think will help you understand what topics you do not understand. This awareness of your shortcomings allows you to take a step back and look for ways to improve them. Improving your language skills will also lend itself to improving your reading. After all, the better you can apply language yourself, the better you will be at reading and identifying the other applications that people use for the same purpose. For instance, understanding a semi-colon and how to use it requires knowledge of what constitutes an independent clause. Improving your grammar in this way boosts your reading comprehension and keeps you from being confused when authors throw weird grammatical structures at you. It will also boost your self-confidence, making you a better writer, conversationalist, or public speaker. Your first impressions will be stronger with greater language skills as well.

Here are 6 exercises to improve your reading speed and comprehension in other ways. Some of these are a review of earlier techniques, others are new.

Size-up the Task

Assess the work you are about to do. Skim the text first and look for important points. Catch the headings and subheadings; read the first and the last paragraphs of several chapters; get accustomed to the writing style unique to each author. Grasp the forest before focusing on the trees. Not only will you keep an eye on the big picture, but you should be able to identify the main ideas after a quick skim.

Ask Questions

As you read through the text, create questions you are wanting to find answers to. Then anticipate finding the answers to your questions. Focus on your interests and what you want to take away from the reading. Skip the irrelevant information. It is impossible to remember everything you read, so learn to pull out what is relevant to your needs. You know exactly what you need to take away from the reading. Then, at the end of the reading, you will have either answered questions, and gained something from it, or you will have more questions, thus, more reading.

Decrease Subvocalization

As discussed earlier in the book, while subvocalization can help with comprehension, it greatly slows your reading speed. When children first learn to read, they whisper the words or say them softly. At the next level, they read silently but still move their lips as if saying each word. As adults, we say the words in our minds—it is called "subvocalization." However, subvocalization does not allow us to read faster because we can only go as fast as we speak. The average speaking rate is about 150 words per minute, while the average reading speed is about 200-300 words per minute. So, to read faster, we need to silence that voice inside. How? Listening to music while reading helps. At first, it will affect your comprehension. But soon you will notice your concentration increases. Paradoxically, the music that distracted you earlier will help you to focus and learn faster. Think about when you put music on as background noise, for when you are doing chores, or at a party, or anywhere else for that matter. Generally, you notice it at first, but then it fades away into the scenery. You only notice it once in a while. The same will happen when you read with music playing.

Read Groups of Words

I mentioned earlier that you should read phrases not words. Here is how you can actually put that into practice. Children learn to read starting with joining syllables. Later, they join words to understand sentences. We often stop there. But, there is another level—absorbing groups of words at once. Remember the columns from chapter five? Grab a pencil and divide the page into 3 columns, so each of them has 2 to 4 words in a row. Try to read them together jumping from one column to another. It is easier than you think. Once you get the hang of it, you will not need the columns. We are just applying the same rule from comprehending words. We do not read every letter but we recognize the whole word. Now, instead of reading separate words, you are reading groups at once.

Quiz Yourself

Ask yourself, "What is the author trying to say? How is this different than other things I have read? How does this relate to other material I know?" When you are making sense of something, you start learning it. Employ this method when you stop in the middle of reading, rather than rereading a section. Summarize what you just read as if you had been stopped by a teacher in class and been given a pop quiz. If it feels right, keep reading.

Do Not Just Consume, Create

Knowledge is not just something you absorb, but rather something that you create as a learner. You develop new meanings, new neural network connections, and new patterns of electro/chemical interactions within you. Learning happens when you integrate your new knowledge, then apply it in some way to enforce a new work process or create something new. Practical application of your newfound knowledge is a great way to practice a new skill.

Take notes and write. Do not type on a computer. While typing your notes into the computer is great for posterity, writing by hand stimulates ideas more effectively. The simple act of holding and using a pen or pencil may seem old-fashioned in this day and age, but just think of all the visionaries it has worked for throughout the years. Not only that, despite the fact that typing is faster than handwriting notes, the multi-functionality of a laptop lends itself to distractions way more than handwriting. Even though it makes taking notes on large amounts of information easier, all it takes is one notification, or one sound, or one errant thought, and a couple clicks later you go down the rabbit hole of distraction. An article from National Public Radio (NPR) cites a study that Psychological Science published, determining that longhand notes forced note-takers to select the things they write down more carefully. So while it is possible that laptop users take down more notes, odds are handwriters take better notes because they identified the most important information while ignoring the less important points. The study tested this by showing TED talks to students about various topics before asking questions about facts, which both groups accomplished equally well. Concept-based questions, however, significantly favored the handwritten notes. The temptation to write things verbatim, that is word by word, was simply too much to overcome when using a laptop.

This was just one hypothesis tested to determine whether the act of taking notes by hand or by typing affected memory and retention. The second allowed students the chance to review the notes they had taken between the lecture and the test. Handwritten notes still yielded stronger results. The conclusion was that taking notes by hand requires 'mental lifting' on the part of the brain, fostering comprehension and retention. Typing notes induces a more mindless, get-everything-down-while-I-can approach. This study removed the variable of distraction, disconnecting the Internet on each laptop. Even the most diligent students can get distracted, and most waste 40 percent of class time on things unrelated to the lecture or their coursework. One study of law school students showed nearly 90% of those with laptops used them for at least five minutes to do activities with no relation to the coursework. Maybe even more shocking, 60% spend half the class distracted. Long story short, the overwhelming evidence suggests that old-fashioned pen and paper benefits your retention.

Skimming Motions Recommended by Evelyn Wood

Beyond that, other experts offer strategies and techniques that lead to greater reading speed and do not sacrifice retention. Many consider Evelyn Wood as the pioneer who popularized speed reading with her

Seven Day Speed Reading and Learning Program. Similar to this book, she promises things like doubling current speeds of reading, improving reading comprehension and recall, sharpening concentration, and notably, since she gears her book toward students, adhering to deadlines. She asks readers to use a series of unorthodox hand motions to keeps their eyes engaged and moving as they peruse the information on the page.

Motion 1: Altered Metaguiding

Palm on the page, fingers together but relaxed, all flat, you move your hand along the page much as you would with regular meta-guiding. Use your hand to pace your eyes. The major between her advice and the meta-guiding we've discussed in prior chapters lies in how you transition between lines. Wood encourages lifting your fingers above the page ¼ to ½ an inch, no more or less, and diagonally bringing your hand to the place where the next line starts, repeating this motion all the way down the page.

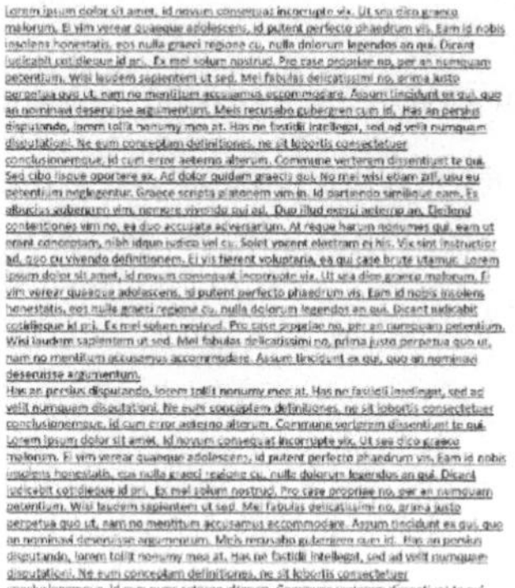

Motion 2: S-shape

The second motion she describes is an S-like motion down the page, fluidly moving between the sides of the page without jumpiness and skipping a line or two in the process. The motions she describes seem to increase in difficulty.

Motion 3: ?-Shape

The third motion involves a similar motion as the first, but instead of tracing lines, you trace the lines down the page in question mark shape.

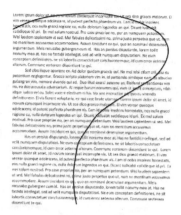

Motion 4: X-Shape

As the fourth motion, Woods suggests using an X-shape, starting at the top left part of the page and moving diagonally about five lines down to the right margin. Once you reach the right margin, move your finger up two lines of text and repeat the first motion in the opposite direction (to the left margin of the page). Again, you'll move up two to three lines, and move down diagonally five lines. Effectively, you'll repeat these zig-zag, "X" motions until you reach the bottom of the page.

Motion 5: The Loop

The fifth motion makes a loop and follows a similar path to the X, only the motions are smoother, more fluid. Imagine making a figure 8. Create these loops, moving down the page five lines and circling back up a couple (from left to right then right to left) until you reach the bottom of the page.

Motion 6: L-Shape

The last she motion she suggests is the L-motion, which would confuse anyone who does not know how to write in cursive. Similar to the loop motion, you move down the page with loops. However, rather than moving to the right margin diagonally down the page, you read straight across a line before looping up and moving down five lines diagonally on the backstroke (to the left margin). For those interested, she provides four more, the horseshoe, U, brush, and half-moon. For risk of losing you further in this digression. I will provide the diagrams and move along.

Another similar meta-guiding technique, much more simplistic than the elaborate hand motions Evelyn Wood uses, involves using a blank white index card. It makes sense. The index card helps to focus your eyes as they track words along the page. This improved focus is coupled with an increase in retention. However, you must be careful doing this not to inadvertently regress. To do as much, you can follow the advice of the article from *Fast Company*. Place the index card above the line you want to read. This not only prevents your eyes from returning up the page, it encourages and even forces them to continue moving down. This adds a barrier to regression, as you must conscientiously remove the index card from preceding text to look over any information you already passed. There is a small catch, however. This above-the-line index card technique does not work too well for reading on a computer since you have to hold your arm out for long periods of time. Even though the index card weighs next to nothing, your arm will get tired before long and keep you from using the technique. Better to not do it at all and save yourself the frustration. Plus, it looks a little ridiculous. In any case, if you are reading for speed, you are much better off reading from a paper source anyway, since on-screen text slows your reading by about 25%.

Other Meta-Guiding Techniques

Sticking with the theme of using a meta-guiding visual pacer, Kwik offers nine more tricks to reading faster and mastering information overload in an article for *Alive.com* in 2017.

First, he suggests visiting an optometrist to get your eyes checked, if you've not done so recently. If not, he says, ensure that your eyesight is at its full potential. Use your prescription glasses or reading glasses.

Next, he emphasizes the importance of finding an appropriate reading place. This often means striking a balance between sleep-inducing comfort and distracting levels of alertness. You could opt to recline with blankets and pillows, but you'd likely fall asleep before you get far. On the other hand, you could blast the A/C, but too much cold would be distracting. Instead, you want to be comfortable, but alert. Keep the room cold, which supports alertness, but not so cold it's distracting. Use a pillow if you need, but don't recline or lay down, as too much relaxation leads to drowsiness.

Another point Kwik makes is that you should find positive anchors that can influence your reading since they can reinforce good self-images about yourself as a reader and discredit bad ones you may have developed along the way. Positivity calms your nerves and relaxes you, essential components to taking in information. Many of these positive anchors involve relaxation and comfort, but they likewise help maintain attentiveness. Try using natural light, for example. You strain your eyes when you read in dim or fluorescent light. Kill the lamps and overhead lights, pop down beside a window, open the curtains, and let the sunlight settle on the pages. In absence of that, some lightbulbs can mimic natural light. Playing music close to a regular heartbeat, about 60 beats per minute, can similarly relax your body and induce a heightened state of learning. The best relaxation method, perhaps, is sitting up straight with good posture to avoid strain on muscles and draw long, deep breaths. Try using a 3-2-4 breathing technique, inhaling through your nose for three seconds, holding for two seconds, and exhaling for four seconds. This keeps your brain well-fueled and running at peak capacity. Related, keeping your book upright will discourage hunching over and promote a direct facing of the page. Staying hydrated will help your brain too, as it functions less effectively when dehydrated. Not only that, your stomach will try to trick you into eating, when in reality, you are just thirsty. Keeping water near you will lessen your trips to the kitchen to snack and keep you focused on the task at hand.

Right Brain and Left Brain Distinctions

Kwik's last point, as it pertains to visual pacing: Use your whole brain. Meta-guide your reading with your left hand to engage your right brain, balancing out your neural function and enriching your reading experience. Any person familiar with left brain versus right brain science will tell you that this makes sense. Children, particularly those who have been diagnosed with dyslexia, struggle when learning how to read because elementary teaching methods cater more to left brain processes. Rather than learning to read the word by addressing each part and arriving at the whole, right-brained students do the opposite. They learn by seeing the whole word and then dissecting it into its component parts. This means that they learn the word based on how it looks, "sight word" approach, rather than how it sounds. Phonics help these children very little since the process involves identifying parts of words that are or sound the same or different. On a big-picture scale, right brain processes lean on context rather than sequence. Left brain students generally read each word in a systematic and orderly fashion, gradually developing an understanding of the passage as they put together words to construct meaning based on each word as a part of the whole. Right-brained children, however, will take multiple words and sentences before processing them as a whole, then search for context clues and develop a mental image of what each word and sentence means. On a practical rather than pedagogical level, this means incremental exercises like phonics bore right-brained children since there are no smaller units to divide them into. They would prefer to learn through real, meaningful books. To borrow an analogy, left brain students may be more likely to want to learn the exact movements and techniques involved in swimming before even getting themselves wet. Right-brained children, however, would be more inclined to dive right into the pool and figure out the finer details later.

Engaging your right brain just as much as, if not more than, your left will take advantage of the tendency to read from an overview perspective, looking at the global picture of what you read to ascertain the overall context. Like a right-brained child, this will include missing details, skipping words, skimming quickly, and not wanting to stop and sound out words. After gaining enough information from the reading to establish an overall picture of the messages, themes, and points conveyed, the right-brained child moves on, leaving the nonessential details behind and not wasting time to focus on them. Right brain processes involve the formation of visual clues, and tend to adhere to silent reading, though occasionally they will read aloud to themselves, making Kwik's point about the reading environment that much more important. So good news, right-brained people, your neural tendencies may be a critical factor in your ability to speed read. Left-brained people, fear not. Although we tend to categorize people as left or right-brained, everyone has the capacity to use both sides of the brain. Just because you favor the side that does not naturally do all of these things does not mean that you are incapable of doing them. It may take some more practice and hard work, but you too can master speed reading effectiveness, for which side of the brain you lean toward does not determine the limit of your abilities.

How do you unlock the capabilities of this magical right brain, you ask? The right side of the brain awaits the arrival of textual information via the corpus callosum, says David Butler in his book *Speed Reading with the Right Brain*. Even though most writing about brain function in general address the left brain, the right controls effective comprehension. To get a sense of what exactly that means, concepts and visual images form as a result of right-brain activity. Overall, as evidenced by the explanation before about how different children learn, the right brain looks at entire images or ideas together and deciphers the patterns and connections within the information. Comprising higher order cognitive processing, the right side interprets information at greater speeds and with more holistic attention to the big picture. This explains the reason behind the monopoly of the right brain over imagination, intuition, facial recognition, and artistry. The right brain simply processes data faster and at a higher volume than the left, meaning reading with the left brain is about as useful, as Butler notes, as squeezing information through a straw.

There is more to it than just that. After processing occurs in both and between the right and left side of the brain, the prefrontal cortex takes over. Consciousness resides here, regulating information, modulating impulses, and coordinating data from the other parts of the brain. In this central location, plans get formulated, decisions made, errors spotted, and habits broken. Most importantly for the exercise of reading, working memory operates in the prefrontal cortex. This is not a perfect system since emotions can affect this area of the brain. That does not have to be a bad thing though, since dopamine, the neurotransmitter that conveys joy and pleasure in the brain, serves as a primer for action and actually strengthens its informational signals, something Butler intentionally points out in the book. Repeated, rhythmic, structured, and easily visualized information aid the prefrontal cortex in remembering information easier.

So, to engage your right brain, Martha Beck offers some exercises to wake that portion of your brain that gets somewhat overlooked in our hyper-rational world. First, she recommends signing your name in every way you can think of. Right to left, upside down, backward and upside down, every direction should be explored to the best of your ability. Second, have a bilateral conversation by writing a question with your right hand and then answering it with your left hand and whatever pops into your mind, regardless of which hand is dominant. Your non-dominant hand will almost certainly write shakily, but do not worry, that is not the point. What is important, though is noticing that your left hand has its own personality. It may sound strange, and it kind of is, but what may be stranger is that your right brain knows things you do not know that you know. It assesses your physical and mental feelings, often offering solutions.

Learning new moves will help your right brain activate since the motions will be unfamiliar to it. Having a hard time thinking of something? Beck uses the example of walking, but instead of swinging your arms opposite your legs, swing them on the same side. Try it in different variations, backward, closing your eyes, any that you can think of that is hard but attainable. Then, throw the kitchen sink at it. In this case, once you activate your right brain, start reading at a blistering pace, faster than you thought you could before. In other applications, you can try to tackle a problem that has been irking you. Instead of stewing over that problem, with your right brain activated, read a few different things, relax, do chores, or anything other than mull over the problem. Do, though, engage it intermittently before dropping it and continuing to do anything else. According to Beck, this provokes epiphanies, similar to eureka moments on television. By engaging more ideas through activities, your brain comes up with the first few potential solutions that may not be any good. Encouraging the brain to churn out solutions yields more and more of them, particularly when the right brain takes over. Rather than being the end goal, activating the right brain for speed reading allows you to deposit more information in that part of your brain. When you activate it again to solve a problem, the information you obtain speed reading with the right side of your brain should be there and become an important factor in increasing your speed reading effectiveness.

Triage-based Reading

Abby Marks Beale believes that choosing the text and picking your battles may be the most important factor in your speed reading effectiveness. Given your limited time, regardless of your speed reading prowess, you need to make choices about what you have time to read and what you do not. Similar to an emergency room, some things, like a heart attack, get precedence over others, such as indigestion, to keep with the example she uses. In other words, you need to perform triage on your reading list. In your large pile of books and articles to be read, you have some heart attacks and some indigestion cases. Identifying the heart attacks advances you further in your reading than the indigestion cases do. That is not to say you should not read books that are not important. Indigestion cases need to be resolved as well. They just have lower priority.

Purpose Setting

Not only should you have a firm idea of what reading is more important, Beale also recommends you know exactly what you want to get out of the reading by having questions readily available that will comprise your purpose in reading. These questions guide your reading and actively engage you with it by seeking out the answers. She calls this "Purpose-Setting" and writes 8-10 questions down on whatever index card or notebook she has available before opening the book. She takes it one step even further, saying that reading alone does not suffice. According to Beale, you need to apply what you read in order to best retain it. My high school English teacher would give us a word of the day before every class. Without fail, every day she said we need to use it three times before we own the word and can use it for ourselves. Similarly, knowledge without application does not get you far. To take full advantage of your reading you need to manifest it into the real-world in some way. Beale offers a litmus of being able to add three tasks to your to-do or projects list that reflect what you have gained from the reading. Reviewing the list to reflect on how well you adapted the reading to your life should relate back to your purpose-setting step and demonstrate a new skill or piece of knowledge.

Assessing your progress, be it in a sort of abstract way that Beale does, or in a more tangible process like the PX Project, a single three-hour-long cognitive experiment, is necessary to your overall experience. Without figuring out where you end up, you do not truly understand your improvements, which could be a reading speed increase of up to 386 percent as in the case of Tim Ferriss. The results of the PX Project are astounding, almost too good to be true. To showcase the efficacy of the project, it comprised speakers of five different languages and incorporated dyslexics. Each of them underwent conditioning that produced reading speeds of highly technical material at a rate of 3,000 words per minute, or 10 pages every minute, 1 page every six seconds. The PX Project bases its methods on a basic understanding of the human visual system, eliminating inefficiencies while increasing speed, without the cost of retention. Ferriss outlines the mechanism of the project in a series of exercises in an article for the Huffington Post. The target areas, minimizing fixations, eliminating regression and back-skipping, and using conditioning drills to maximize horizontal peripheral vision span and the words you register in each fixation, will be familiar to you from the previous pages in this book.

The first technique entails reading two lines in one second with the assistance of a tracker or a pacer, regardless of comprehension, throughout the page. The second expands your perception by beginning one word in from the first word of each line and ending one word from the last, again disregarding comprehension. Ferriss prompts the reader to repeat this task twice more, once using the second word in from the beginning and end of each line, and the other using the third word in on each end, once more ignoring comprehension. He then asks the reader to calculate their new words per minute reading speed. He qualifies this by saying that even though you can read at rates up to triple your previous, you should not use this ability to read three things. Instead, read the same thing three times, and bolster your comprehension.

Wade Cutler promises to *Triple Your Reading Speed* in his so-named book, spending the first thirty or so pages on your current reading skills and the blocks to achieving higher reading speeds. He identifies many of the same things that this book has: failing to preview whatever material in front of you, wasteful eye movements and regressions, poor vision span, vocalization, and subvocalization. General vocalization is not one we talked about much, but includes lipping, tongue warbling, jawing, adam's appling, and diaphragming, various manifestations of reading along inaudibly. He adds more miscellaneous weaknesses, such as pointing/marking, hand-scanning, and slow page turning. While Cutler spends a lot of time on the impediments to speed reading, he has just as many drills to increase your reading speed. From following the middle of three columns of letters while reading from left to right, to progressively more complicated variations, he follows similar eye span increasing theories as Cole and Frank. He expands the range of the letters and jumbles them up into groups of three and four. The columns increase to as many as seven, while the innermost columns get more and more complicated. He then gives the reader drills in the same model to learn pacing and block reading. Shifting to a thin, newspaper-style column, Cutler provides a more practical application of skills. The goal here is one fixation per line. He then ups the difficulty to one fixation per two lines.

Cutler introduces in the next part of the book something he calls the Two Stop Method, resembling something like an S or a Z. Repeating the trend of widening the columns, he first makes your eyes bounce back and forth between two wide ones. They slowly come together as the columns widen. Modulating there after, this is designed to exercise your eyes and help them track consistently between columns. It closely resembles the Eye-Hop method that Ron Cole developed. As a test, Cutler provides excerpts from readings to illustrate his point so that you can apply your newfound skills instantly and test them to see how well you picked them up. He adds a poem from Edgar Allan Poe, the well-known *The Cask Amontillado*, *A Short History of the Civil War*, a chapter from *Treasure Island*, another from *The Time Machine*, *Dr. Jekyll and Mr. Hyde*, and *Money Signs*. Each progresses in length and difficulty, and the tests mimic reading comprehension quizzes from a high school class. He assigns book-length features to give the reader a list to follow and more tests to determine their reading ability.

Chapter Summary

- To keep up with the accelerated creation of information, reading can be your weapon in the arms race of knowledge, and reading

113

this far has gotten you one step closer. Here are six more tips to further advance your speed reading.

- Measure your task before you tackle it. Do not go into it blind. Take a good look at the text you are about to read and make mental notes about what you can expect.

- Ask questions while you read. Odds are the author intentionally made you curious so that he or she can satisfy that curiosity later in the text. Not only that, it will help you keep track of the big ideas and perhaps leave you with questions that will lead you to more reading down the line.

- Decrease subvocalization. Your reading speed is much faster than your speaking speed. When you speak the words, even cognitively, you limit your potential. Silencing that voice can boost your rate of reading. Do not worry about comprehension because at this point you are employing other tactics to compensate for any you lose.

- Read groups of words. Divide each page into three or four columns with a pencil and practice jumping through them in sequential order, line by line. Just do not use this on a book you can not mark up.

- Quiz yourself as you go to keep your memory fresh. Bounce around with your questions and make connections to as many points in the reading as you can.

- On that theme, create as you go. Reference related reading and develop new associations that your brain can follow. Knowledge is not just absorbed, it is created. Active reading facilitates this.

- Take notes by hand. Studies show this helps memory retention much more than typing at a keyboard. If you are still skeptical, think of the countless people who hand wrote things before the invention of the computer or typewriter. You will find some pretty smart people.

- In her book How to Fly with Your Hands, Evelyn Wood issued one of the first speed reading guides in 1959 with some interesting hand motions. She designed them to move your eye and track it across the page in different manners. This sets the same goal as meta-guiding, to pace your eyes across the page and standardize your reading speed.

- Try placing an index card on the page as a meta-guide. Below the line you are currently reading is an acceptable method, but be careful not to regress to any of the information you just read above it. A more effective tactic would be to place the index card on the line above the one you are trying to read, so that your regressions will be greatly reduced, if not eliminated. Also, this will force your eyes to keep moving forward and down the page, increasing your progress compared to the alternate placement. The only catch, the index card does not work well with a computer screen, since you have to hold the index card out with your arm stretched. It can tire you out quickly, but that is okay because reading on paper rather than a screen keeps you from losing 25% of your speed anyway.

- Jim Kwik, who I mentioned earlier in chapter five, has some interesting tidbits that deal with more than the act of reading. The environment in which you read affects your reading about as much as anything. So too does your posture, and something as basic as how you hold the book. Staying hydrated will have an effect too. His most insightful point may be the way he suggests to use your brain, that is, to fully engage it. Reading is often associated with the left brain because of the logic that it relies on. However, in analyzing how right-brained children learn, and specifically learn to read, the very things you look to do in speed reading appear. Focusing on the conceptual big picture, missing minor details, skipping words, and most of all, moving on with inessential details behind, all sound like speed reading best practices.

- Engage your right brain when you read. Kwik suggests you use your left hand to meta-guide, potentially an effective method to awaken that side of your brain. However, a more substantial effort to activate your left brain, by signing your name every way you can, having bilateral conversations, learning new moves, then throwing the kitchen sink at it, as Martha Beck advises, will fully activate it. Right brain activation will not necessarily speed up your reading. That is a more conscious choice you make. The byproduct, however, will reveal itself in a higher comprehension of what you speed read since speed reading activities align with right brain ones, as mentioned before.

- Abby Marks Beale encourages you to choose your battles and prioritize the most important reading you want to get done, similar to how an emergency room treats the most important cases first. She recommends you have 8-10 questions before you read to set your purpose and guide you toward your goal for reading whatever it is you have in front of you. Then, actually use what you obtained from the reading because application boosts retention significantly. Like my English teacher used to say, use it three times, and you own it. She referred to the words of the day, but the premise remains the same. Beale adds three tasks to her to-do or project list that reflect her reading. Reviewing the list makes you reflect on what you have added to your life by reading that text.

- Tim Ferriss proclaims the benefits of the PX Project, boasting a 386 percent increase in his reading speed after the 3-hour lesson. Incorporating meta-guiding, visual perception expansion, and grouping of words, he offers techniques that, when repeated enough, result in astounding increases in reading speed. Through a thorough understanding of the human visual system, the PX Project eliminates inefficiencies to increase speed and maintain retention.

- Wade Cutler claims he can triple your reading speed too through a series of techniques that resemble the columns that Steven Frank provides in his book. Cutler, however, varies them by width, number of letters, and difficulty, working your way up from three columns of single letters to passages from novels. Spending a lot of time focusing on how to remove blocks to speed reading, one area Cutler addresses that none of the other experts do is vocalizing. Similar in principle to subvocalizing, it involves ticks or habits readers have that mimic speech. He identifies movements of the lips, tongue, jaw, adam's apple, and even as far down as your diaphragm. These have the same effect as subvocalization, slowing down your reading in some circumstances

CONCLUSION

Pause a moment. Think back to your mindset as you opened this book. You have come quite a long way. You quite possibly began this journey to speed reading prowess with a vague idea of what speed reading entailed. After reading, you learned about some of the benefits speed reading can bring you. The range is far and wide, from simply being able to take in more information to boosting your confidence, advancing your career, or improving your meditation practices, whether you know it or not. I gave you a preliminary look at what you can expect from this book, and what gains you may be able to make by this point here, the end. Only you know the truth of this. I hope that you remained engaged, applied the techniques, and tracked your progress. At the start, you may have held onto some myths about speed reading, which we debunked right away in chapter two. Namely, they were that you can read 10,000 words per minute, subvocalization inhibits you in your quest to read faster (it does, but not you need not worry about eliminating it until you're at an advanced learning stage), and that you automatically practice reading faster when you read normally.

I encouraged you to embrace whatever reading ability you had coming into this book. An understanding and evaluation of yourself allows you to analyze how you can improve most, and the areas that need more focus. Being honest with yourself can be challenging, and so can reading, particularly since it is not a factory default setting to the human condition. With this as an abstract baseline, chapter four gave you a more concrete one by calculating your reading speed. It also gave you a benchmark by providing speeds for a variety of different reading levels.

Chapter five started the transformative process of turning you into a speed reader. It gave you all sorts of techniques to try when you practice your speed reading, from first and foremost setting a goal, to skimming, cutting down on subvocalization, reading phrases, meta-guiding, rapid serial visualization, avoiding regression and limiting fixations. These may have originally boosted your reading speed significantly, but you may have noticed a drop in comprehension.

Chapter six remedied that by giving you counters to a drop in retention. These included visualization, allowing some words and phrases to go because they were too complicated, expanding your vocabulary, and playing the recall game.

These tips and tricks alone are not enough, though, as chapter seven lays out. One of the best ways to get better at reading is to do more of it. The one caveat is that you have to read mindfully. A good place to start is books that are easy to read, as the input hypothesis developed by Stephen Krashen suggests that texts with words that fall under a threshold of 95 percent knowledge make a commitment to continue reading even more difficult. This chapter gave some helpful ways to build a routine for reading, like focusing on the building blocks of the habit, making it easier for you to start, reading books because you enjoy them, keeping your options open by switching books and building up to harder books by expanding your foundation first through research.

Keeping track of your reading may be most important, especially if you need the positive reinforcement to keep up your habit. There are so many ways, first and foremost timing your reading regularly to keep checkpoints of where you are. A good old-fashioned reading log in a planner or notebook will never fail to keep you on track, as long as you keep up with it. In the digital age, more and more productivity and functionality can shift to the online forum, where Goodreads, Spreadsheets, Trello, and Pinterest boards can document your reading and engage you with other readers or more content. When in doubt, to either supplement or replace any of these, a tried and true pile of books can make an adequate reading log, especially if you like to juggle multiple books and keep one or two to look forward to handy.

The best way to get through them, and a tactic that many people probably already utilize, skim and scan your reading while retaining the important information. It is important to discredit the misconceptions. Skimming and scanning are not quickly glancing over pages and turning them, expecting information to flow easily and effortlessly. There is an inherent trade-off between speed and retention, but skimming and scanning account for this. It is not a temporary fix, nor does it undermine the author's tone and disrespect their careful word choice. On the contrary, they require a dedicated and mindful approach to any reading. They start with something simple, knowing what you want to get out of it, through pre-reading or your own assessment. Then you read vertically as much, if not more than, horizontally, while putting yourself in the place of the author to figure out the strategies and reasons behind the text. Be selective about what you choose to read, for instance, read the first sentence in a paragraph, but not necessarily every complete sentence or examples.

Lastly, chapter ten should have left you with more advanced methods for speed reading. Staying ahead of the pack in a competitive digital world involves sizing up your tasks, asking questions, decreasing subvocalization, reading groups of words, quizzing yourself, applying your reading by creating knowledge after you read, and taking notes with your hand and not with a computer. A chief strategy among the ones listed in this chapter, and not mentioned in chapter five, is making use of your right brain, which can potentially improve your comprehension several fold. Doing so will allow the information to process through both sides of your brain. The left contributes to logical functions and facilitates your efforts to deposit knowledge into long-term memory banks. The right side of the brain processes information at a substantially faster rate, making it wise and effective to hand over as much information to it, especially as you read for speed. Expert testimonies bolster this chapter and introduce you to unique and constructive methods, building off of some of the ones earlier in the chapter or that resurface from chapter five.

As you may have noticed, these tips build on each other in just that way. Some simple techniques introduced in the exposition of the book come back later in different and more complicated ways. Do not confuse them for the same thing, for instance, meta-guiding with your pen is different from doing so with an index card which is different from using your left hand, or using some seemingly ridiculous hand motions as Evelyn Wood suggests. If you employ these tips in conjunction, you will find yourself reading faster and retaining more without actively trying to do so (although that's beside the point, you should most definitely be actively trying to improve your reading pace). I cannot guarantee that you can now magically be able to read anything you pick up at a rate of

1,500 words per minute. It is not a snap of the fingers that time leaps you into the next morning where you'll roll out of bed, pick up a book, and read it as a superhero would. We've already dispelled such fantastical notions. You yourself need to take charge of your own reading and incorporate the methods, techniques, tips, and tricks I have provided in a way that works best for you. Consider these solutions to your problem, an instruction manual for your project, if you will. But this is a do-it-yourself type of project, and I cannot do it for you. Develop your own routines, rituals, habits, or tendencies. Whatever you do, take note of each of these tips and tricks and work your way up to 1,500 words per minute reading. You have the tools and instructions. Now build your way up to that goal. I have every faith in you.

RESOURCES

Beck, M. (n.d.). Creativity Boost: How to Tap into Right-Brain
Thinking. Retrieved December 23, 2019, from
https://www.oprah.com/spirit/how-to-tap-into-the-right-side-of-
your-brain-martha-beck-advice/all

Booth, A. (2014, February 4). 10 Reasons Why You Should Learn
Speed Reading. Retrieved December 22, 2019, from
https://www.lifehack.org/articles/lifestyle/10-reasons-why-you-
should-learn-speed-reading.html

Burke, S. (2014, March 13). The Spritz app lets you read at 1,000 wpm
-- but at what cost? Retrieved December 22, 2019, from
https://money.cnn.com/2014/03/13/technology/innovation/spritz/

Butler, D. (2017). *Speed Reading with the Right Brain: Learn to Read
Ideas Instead of Just Words.* ? CreateSpace Independent Publishing
Platform.

Capuano, R. (2019, April 23). Right-Brained Reading. Retrieved
December 23, 2019, from
https://www.thehomeschoolmom.com/right-brained-reading/

Cole, R. (2012). *SuperReading for Success: The Groundbreaking,
Brain-Based Program to Improve Your Speed, Enhance Your
Memo ry, and Increase Your Success.* New York: Penguin
Publishing Group.

Cutler, W. E. (1993). *Triple Your Reading Speed*. New York: Prentice Hall.

de Bruijn, O., & Spence, R. (2000). Rapid Serial Visual Presentation: A space-time trade-off in information presentation. Retrieved from https://www.researchgate.net/profile/Oscar_Bruijn2/publication/22 0944929_Rapid_Serial_Visual_Presentation_A_space-timed_trade-off_in_information_presentation/links/09e415112db90c75ed00000 0.pdf

DeRusha, B. (2019, August 23). 10 Speed Reading Apps to Help You Tackle Your TBR. Retrieved December 22, 2019, from https://bookriot.com/2018/10/19/best-speed-reading-apps/

Doubek, J. (2016, April 17). Attention, Students: Put Your Laptops Away. Retrieved December 23, 2019, from https://choice.npr.org/index.html?origin=https://www.npr.org/2016 /04/17/474525392/attention-students-put-your-laptops-away

Duggan, G., & Payne, S. (2009). Text skimming: The process and effectiveness of foraging through text under time pressure. *Journal of Experimental Psychology: Applied*, *15*(3), 228–242. https://doi.org/10.1037/a0016995

Ferriss, T. (2014, July 13). How I Learned to Read 300 Percent Faster in 20 Minutes. Retrieved December 23, 2019, from https://www.huffpost.com/entry/speed-reading_b_5317784

Frank, S. (1998). *Backpack Series-Speed Reading Secrets (The Backpack Study Series)*. Holbrook, Massachusetts: Adams Media.

Frank, S. D. (1994). *The Evelyn Wood Seven-Day Speed Reading and Learning Program*. Fall River, MA: Fall River Press.

Grothaus, M. (2018, May 24). How to train yourself to become a speed reader. Retrieved December 22, 2019, from https://www.fastcompany.com/40574769/how-to-train-yourself-to-become-a-speed-reader

Halton, M. (2019, April 1). A speed reader shares 3 tricks to help anyone read faster. Retrieved December 22, 2019, from https://ideas.ted.com/a-speed-reader-shares-3-tricks-to-help-anyone-read-faster/

Hammond, B. (2018, March 22). What is the Strengths Perspective? :: Speed Reading Study Explained Better Than Ever. Retrieved January 1, 2020, from https://www.isogostrong.com/strengthsfinder-speed-reading/

Harari, Y. N. (2015). *Sapiens: A Brief History of Humankind*. New York: Harper.

Harry, J. (2018, December 28). 5 Things Holding Your Reading Speed Back. Retrieved December 22, 2019, from https://medium.com/@studyfast/5-things-holding-your-reading-speed-back-aac6405fc5c0

Kaufman, J. (n.d.). 10 Days to Faster Reading - Abby Marks-Beale. Retrieved December 22, 2019, from https://joshkaufman.net/10-days-to-faster-reading/

Kraushaar, J., & Novak, D. (2010). Examining the Affects of Student Multitasking with Laptops during the Lecture. *Journal of Information Systems Education*, *21*(2), 241–251. Retrieved from https://eric.ed.gov/?id=EJ893903

Kump, P. (1998). *Breakthrough Rapid Reading* (Revised ed.). New

York: Prentice Hall Press.

Kwik, J. (n.d.). Kwik Brain 007: How to Read Faster. Retrieved December 22, 2019, from https://jimkwik.com/kwik-brain-007/

Kwik, J. (2017, January 21). 10 Tricks for Speed-Reading (That Will Save You So Much Time). Retrieved December 22, 2019, from https://www.alive.com/lifestyle/speed-read-like-a-boss/

Larsen, L. (n.d.). *Does Speed Reading Improve College Student's Retention Level and Comprehension?* Retrieved from http://leannlarsen.com/Portfolio/Speed%20Reading%20Research.pdf

Macalister, J. (2010). Speed reading courses and their effect on reading authentic texts: A preliminary investigation. *Reading in a Foreign Language, 22*(1), 104–116. Retrieved from http://nflrc.lll.hawaii.edu/rfl/April2010/articles/macalister.pdf

May, C. (2014, June 3). A Learning Secret: Don't Take Notes with a Laptop. Retrieved December 23, 2019, from https://www.scientificamerican.com/article/a-learning-secret-don-t-take-notes-with-a-laptop/

Montgomery, C. (2018, November 4). How to Improve Reading Comprehension: 8 Expert Tips. Retrieved December 22, 2019, from https://blog.prepscholar.com/how-to-improve-reading-comprehension

Nation, P. (2005). Reading Faster. *PASAA, 36*, 21–37.

National Research Council. (2012). *Improving Adult Literacy Instruction: Developing Reading and Writing.* https://doi.org/10.17226/13468

Nelson, B. (2012, July 30). Do You Read Fast Enough To Be Successful? Retrieved January 1, 2020, from https://www.forbes.com/sites/brettnelson/2012/06/04/do-you-read-fast-enough-to-be-successful/#2db68dab462e

Olson, S. (2015, January 7). The Science of Speed Reading; Benefits And Consequences Of Reading 1,000 Pages In 10 Hours. Retrieved December 22, 2019, from https://www.medicaldaily.com/science-speed-reading-benefits-and-consequences-reading-1000-pages-10-hours-316828

Peterson, D. (2019, July 3). How to Read Faster and Have More Study Time. Retrieved December 23, 2019, from https://www.thoughtco.com/how-to-read-faster-31624

Rayner, K., Schotter, E. R., Masson, M. E. J., Potter, M. C., & Treiman, R. (2016). So Much to Read, So Little Time. *Psychological Science in the Public Interest, 17*(1), 4–34. https://doi.org/10.1177/1529100615623267

Rodrigues, J. (2019, September 6). 5 Reasons Why Speed Reading Is Good For Your Brain. Retrieved December 23, 2019, from https://www.irisreading.com/5-reasons-why-speed-reading-is-good-for-your-brain/

Scott, S. J. (2019, December 17). How to Read Faster: 9 Steps to Increase Your Speed in 2020. Retrieved December 22, 2019, from https://www.developgoodhabits.com/how-to-read-faster/

Super-Speed Reading. (n.d.). Retrieved December 10, 2019, from https://tvtropes.org/pmwiki/pmwiki.php/Main/SuperSpeedReading

The Mind Tools Content Team. (n.d.). Speed Reading: – How to

Absorb Information Quickly and Effectively. Retrieved December 22, 2019, from https://www.mindtools.com/speedrd.html

Thielen, J., Grochowski, P., Perpich, D., & Samuel, S. (2016). *Speed Reading and Reading Retention Workshop - Poster and Active Learning Exercises*. Ann Arbor, MI: University of Michigan Library.

Trafton, A. (2014, January 16). In the blink of an eye. *MIT News*. Retrieved from http://news.mit.edu/2014/in-the-blink-of-an-eye-0116

Ways, M. (2019a, April 2). Reading Comprehension Strategies. Retrieved December 22, 2019, from https://www.speedreadinglounge.com/reading-comprehension-strategies

Ways, M. (2019b, November 6). Skimming and Scanning – 4 Strategies. Retrieved December 22, 2019, from https://www.speedreadinglounge.com/skimming-and-scanning

Young, S. (2019, August 18). I Was Wrong About Speed Reading: Here are the Facts. Retrieved December 22, 2019, from https://www.scotthyoung.com/blog/2015/01/19/speed-reading-redo/

YOUR FREE GIFT

Thank you again for purchasing this book. As an additional thank you, you will receive an e-book, as a gift, and completely free.

This includes a fun and interactive daily checklist and workbook to help boost your productivity through simple activities. Life can get so busy, and this bonus booklet gives you easy and efficient tips and prompts to help you get more done, every day.

You can get the bonus booklet as follows:

To access the secret download page, open a browser window on your computer or smartphone and enter: **bonus.john-r-torrance.com**

You will be automatically directed to the download page.

Please note that this bonus booklet may be only available for download for a limited time.

Made in the USA
Middletown, DE
09 August 2020